TREKKING PEBBLED PATHS WITH JESUS

Devotional Guide
Lessons from the Father Series, Book 2

S.D. Simms

M Zion Ridge Press
Books Off the Beaten Path

www.MtZionRidgePress.com

Mt Zion Ridge Press LLC
295 Gum Springs Rd, NW
Georgetown, TN 37366

https://www.mtzionridgepress.com

ISBN 13: 978-1-962862-91-2

Published in the United States of America
Publication Date: September 15, 2025

Copyright: © 2024 Sharon D. Simms

Editor-In-Chief: Michelle Levigne
Executive Editor: Tamera Lynn Kraft

Cover art design by Tamera Lynn Kraft
Cover Art Copyright by Mt Zion Ridge Press LLC © 2025

TABLE OF CONTENTS

JESUS IS —

ACKNOWLEDGEMENTS

He who began a good work in us will complete it unto the end. I'm persuaded that the Lord has the power to accomplish what He has promised. Praise God from Whom all blessings flow. This work stems from wisdom acquired while trekking through trials and walking the pathway of peace with Jesus. Thank You, Jesus Christ, my Lord and Savior. Great gratitude goes to each person in the Christian writing world for invaluable information offered via conference classes, conversations, and critiques. Amre, Lori, Joy Mass., and Joy Mel, I treasure your loyalty and experience. Kudos to Page 44 Critique Group. You ladies rock! Last but not least, *gracias* to family and friends. Your unconditional love, encouragement, and words of affirmation mean much.

Blessings, Sharon.

ENDORSEMENTS

These pages hold truth, refreshment, and hope for the woman seeking to know and find Jesus in the midst of her everyday life. Sharon so beautifully draws our hearts to God's love and leads us to offer our lives in purposeful service to Him. I'm so thankful for this approachable and relevant resource.

Katy McCown
Mother of six, speaker
Best-selling author of *She Belongs: Finding Your Place in the Body of Christ*

Trekking Pebbled Paths with Jesus journeys the reader through forty days of discovering biblical insights about our Lord and Savior. Through Scripture and practical application, a believer grows in understanding how Jesus longs for us to walk through life.

DiAnn Mills, author
Diannmills.com
Canyon of Deceit – Tyndale September 2025

Sharon Simms has crafted a devotional of gratitude and love for our Savior. The verses she has chosen to expand and the personal stories give real-life examples that bring the scriptures to life. She then helps us think through what we've read with insightful questions in the journal sections. Over and over as I read it, I murmured the words, "Thank You, Jesus." Simms speaks truth, and this book shares it with the rest of us in a gorgeous, uplifting way.

Paula Peckham, award-winning author
President of the DFW chapter of American Christian Fiction Writers

INTRODUCTION

Life presents rocky challenges that cause pain. Don't trek alone. Jesus will walk with, cover, coach, and comfort us on our life journey. Imagine the discomfort and hurt suffered from walking barefoot on a rock-riddled path versus the soft cushion of green pastures. Shielding our feet in shoes deters some pain. Jesus Christ is the divine covering who helps and aids us in trekking terrain pebbled with problems, trials, and grief. He guides us safely to God's presence. Don't do life alone. Trek pebbled paths with Jesus Christ, our Lord and Savior.

This workbook contains forty-one devotionals, prayers, and poems penned to aid readers in recognizing Jesus' voice and following Him. The same voice and presence coaxed the Apostle Peter to step into a storm-ridden sea and drew crowds who traveled myriad paths. People trekked across barren deserts, rock-strewn roads, and across rivers to witness Jesus perform miracles and preach authoritative doctrine. Some throughways were well-worn and wide from frequent use, while others were narrow trails. Each avenue of travel was commonly called a "way." The curious and conscience-stricken, the sick seeking healing, and obstinate opposers sought Christ, the Way, the Truth, and the Life. Citizens from Egypt, Syria, Phoenicia, Greece, and foreigners journeyed on foot, by carriage, or beast. They all trekked toward Jesus on paths pebbled with life's afflictions.

Paul, the apostle commissioned by Jesus, yearned to know the excellence of the knowledge of Christ Jesus. Paul's letter to the church at Philippi stated, "…that I may know Him and the power of His resurrection, and the fellowship of His sufferings…" (Phil. 3:8-10)

SD Simms longs for readers to perceive Jesus as their personal escort to God's presence, acknowledge Him as the very essence of the Father, and relish and rest in the Savior's love and power. When your way is riddled with rough life pebbles, make haste and trek a pathway to peace with Jesus.

PRAYER PAGES

Dedication Prayer

Lord, this offering is dedicated to praise, honor, glorify, and draw others to You. I pray You will take my pitiful attempts and anoint them with abundant favor. I pray blessings on all who have worked to bring these words to print. May the words draw readers in and compel them to search the scriptures. May they sense Your agape love, revel in promises of peace during storms, and know confident assurance of Your ever-presence. Lord, I hope this offering captures a pleasing portrait of Your divine grace, lovingkindness, and long-suffering for those who are broken in spirit, and of contrite heart. Use the book to encourage all who long to live the way we were created to fulfill our purpose. Please bless all who worked to bring these words to print. May Your touch have no limit. Forgive me for procrastinating and getting distracted. My greatest desire is to do Your will. I love You, Lord. I'm so thankful for every blessing. May the hills and valleys I trek lead me on the pathway to Your peace. Amen.

Thanksgiving

I thank You for a brand-new day filled with fresh mercies, grace, and the ability to rise, breathe, and know all my help comes from You. Teach me Your Word and show me how to live for You. I'm thankful, so thankful to feel pain and know I'm in the land of the living. Lord, I have not resisted unto the shedding of blood. Thank You for the creature comforts I don't deserve. May I stand for right and strong against wrong, remembering Your sacrifice for my liberties. Amen.

Prayer for Guidance

Lord, thank You for a new day's dawning. Guide my words, thoughts, and actions. May I represent You well and imitate love, grace, and mercy in daily dealings with Your people. Amen.

Prayer of Comfort

You're a friend acquainted with sorrow and a Son Who has suffered pain. Show me how to comfort others as You have consoled me in hours of loss and grief. May pure love and concern prompt considerate and kind care. Amen.

Morning Prayer

Good morning, Lord! I greet You with a humble and grateful heart for breath in my body, new mercies, fresh grace, and a kingdom perspective. Thank You for every good and perfect gift. May I live, talk, and think to represent You well, edify people, and glorify Your name. Lead me by the

Spirit of truth. Amen.

Prayer for Parents of Prodigals

Lord, help me to make amends to the child You gave me to steward. The past spans like a sea rolling with hurts, miscommunication, and sin that separates us. Break down walls of unforgiveness, resentment, and suppressed pain with the light of Your love. If it be Thy will, allow an opportunity for a new creation to speak sincere words of repentance. Draw Your prodigal to You. Restore our earthly parent-child fellowship fresh as the dawn of a new day. Amen.

Prayer for the Caretaker

May I love and minister to the one You have placed in my care, as I pray others will see after me. Keep my heart compassionate, my mind strong and stayed on You. Lord, may I be diligent in tending to my needs of sunshine, healthy eating habits, and respite time with You. Amen.

Prayer of the Sick

Great Physician, you can speak a word or touch as You did Peter's mother-in-law, and You will heal me. I have faith. Paul asked three times for deliverance from an affliction. You gave him grace to withstand. I trust You, Lord. May Your power be made perfect in my weakness.
You're a rewarder of those who diligently seek You. Your will be done, Amen.

Prayer for Writers

Lord, I'm a vessel You have gifted with a hunger to tell others about You through writing. Keep me humble and focused on the goal. Bind the enemy, my flesh, and cares of this world from thwarting the purpose for which You created me. May the words I pen and the life I live glorify Your name. Thank You for trusting me with Your story. Amen.

Prayer for Teachers

Lord, teach me wondrous works of Your law. Hide Your Word in my heart. Fill my cup with abundant grace and love for each student sent into the classroom. Grant me divine perspective and spiritual power from on high to reach those hardened by hurt, distrust, and environment. May I show unconditional love. Strengthen my physical body and sharpen my intellect to pour knowledge into Your people. Amen.

WHAT IF — A REFLECTION

What if each new day we rose and knelt in humble gratitude for the blessings of life, fresh mercies, grace, and provident care?

Not one adverse word, groan, or frown would be displayed anywhere.

What if we greeted family, friends, pets, and foreigners with sincere love and affection, not marred or affected by morning blues, circumstances, or the past?

Words, actions, and attitudes that lined up with the fruit of the Spirit and never ceased to last.

What if we dared not think about I or me but shifted to a different perspective and focused on what's best for You, they, and we?

What if every authority figure sought wisdom from the Lord, asking Him to lead and guide?

Think of the positive changes in this world that are not bound with selfish and arrogant pride.

What if we, as a nation, remembered and reverted to our Pledge of Allegiance, "One nation, under God, indivisible, with liberty and justice for all"?

What if love conquered hate, generosity overcame envy, connection replaced comparison, and grace replaced unforgiveness?

What if, my friends, we each remembered God's great grace came from heaven with a sweet infant's face?

He dwelt among His people, teaching and preaching again and again.

God's Grace died on a cross to save us from our sins.

JESUS IS — THE REDEEMER

In whom we have redemption, the forgiveness of sins. (Col. 1:14)

One of my favorite childhood shopping trips was to the Green Stamp store. Back in the day, certain grocers rewarded customers with stamps for qualified purchase amounts. The stamps were pasted in books and redeemed for merchandise at stores that only accepted stamps.

Days before the shopping excursion, my brother and I pored through a catalog that listed each available item. Imagine a child-like wonder at buying items with stamp books instead of money. Money couldn't purchase merchandise at the stamp store, nor could it pay the debt for humanity's sins. We needed a perfect sacrifice to redeem us from eternal damnation. God's Son fulfilled the qualifications required to redeem us. He is our Redeemer.

Easton's Bible Dictionary defines *Redeemed* (Greek form is Apolutrosis)[1] as the purchase back of something or someone lost by a ransom payment. Romans 3:23 confirms that all have sinned and fallen short of God's glory. God demonstrated His love for us by sending Jesus Christ as the righteous ransom for our redemption.

Centuries ago, Christ our Redeemer commissioned an apostle named Paul to share the good news of salvation with Jews and Gentiles. Paul was imprisoned in Rome for sharing the gospel (good news of Christ) when he received disturbing news: False teachers (heretics) bombarded Christians at Colossae with words refuting Christ's preeminence (supremacy). The apostle wrote a letter in haste, addressed to the Colossians and the church at Laodicea, which laid out irrefutable proof of Jesus' identity. Verses 12-13 of Colossians Chapter 1 outline man's position as believers and unbelievers. Colossians 1:14 (KJV) "In whom we have redemption through his blood, *even* the forgiveness of sins," validates Jesus' blood as the crimson cord that releases and washes all the guilt and stain away. Jesus redeemed (purchased our freedom, paid our sin debt) the final destiny for those who confess Him as Lord and Savior. Holy God loved us so much that He sent His only begotten Son to rescue and redeem us. Jesus, our Redeemer, revives us inside out.

Most of the time, we left the Green Stamp Store with household items our parents chose. On rare occasions, they allowed us to take home a treasured toy. Imagine our excitement and joy with those new possessions, but material resources are non-permanent. Redemption through Jesus Christ, the greatest gift of all, is much sweeter and lasts forever. We become children of Abba Father.

Let's be intentional in illustrating our redeemed status through our actions and speech. Remember that someone is always watching our conduct. Pray and seek God's guidance each day. Always be ready to give an answer for the hope that bubbles in you. (1 Pet. 3:15)

Prayer: *Jesus, Redeemer, Lord Almighty, we praise You for shedding Your blood to wash our souls stain-free. Amen.*

---

[1] https://www.biblestudytools.com/dictionaries/eastons-bible-dictionary/redemption.html

Jesus Is — The Redeemer
Worksheet

… in whom we have redemption, the forgiveness of sins. (Col. 1:14)

1. Define *redeem* using your own words.

2. List someone or something you have redeemed and a reason for your decision.

3. Explain why God forgave us after Jesus redeemed us.

Additional Scriptures
In him we have redemption through his blood, the forgiveness of sins, in accordance with the riches of God's grace … (Eph. 1:7)

JESUS IS — A FRIEND LIKE DORCAS

In Joppa, there was a disciple named Tabitha (in Greek her name is Dorcas); she was always doing good and helping the poor. (Acts 9:36)

What if every woman comprehended that God created her unique with love, character, and skills, not to compete but to complement, connect, inspire, and impact the world around her? Imagine the positive results near and far. What if every woman loved and lived like Dorcas, a disciple of Jesus?

Tabitha, aka Dorcas, a female follower of Christ, encompassed godliness in conduct, charitable deeds, and service borne out of love. *Tabhyetha*, the Aramaic version of her name, means 'gazelle,' which is *Dorcas* in Greek. Luke described the disciple as "full of good works." He granted us a glimpse in Acts 9 of how Dorcas used her sewing skills to design and create clothing for all the widows, not just a few. As a learner of Jesus, she loved God with all her heart and mind and her neighbor as herself. We can imagine Dorcas delivered prayer and encouragement, along with clothing. Perhaps the community-conscious learner of Christ inspired young, old, and in-between by simply utilizing a skill to attend to the needs in her view and scope of talent. Along the way, she built relationships. Dorcas's service reflected a life dedicated to following Christ as a graceful gazelle.

Gazelles are slender animals like antelopes that travel in herds without a leader and have reflective coats. They run at speeds of forty miles per hour. Tabitha surrendered to the Lord. She sewed garments at a swift pace and distributed them in a tender, sincere manner.

Again, I pose a question from the first paragraph. What if women perceived the unmeasured resources of support, friendship, and accountability we have in one another? Opportunities abound to employ your natural expertise. Jump in and help. Don't be concerned with who gets the credit. Teach the gracious love of Jesus by example.

Prayer: Lord, show me how to follow, serve, and use the gifts placed in me to help others. Amen.

Additional Scriptures
Religion that God our Father accepts as pure and faultless is this: to look after orphans and widows in their distress and to keep oneself from being polluted by the world. (Jms. 1:27)

Jesus Is—A Friend Like Dorcas
Worksheet

1. Name a Dorcas in your life.

2. Who would you like to be a Dorcas for?

3. What talents could you use to help others?

4. What might each part of a garment represent from a Christian seamstress to a widow?

The sleeves _____

The bodice _____

The outer cloak _____

JESUS IS – THE HOPE OF GLORY

To them God has chosen to make known among the Gentiles the glorious riches of this mystery, which is Christ in you, the hope of glory. (Col. 1:27)

In the *Oxford Dictionary*[2] hope is defined as a confident expectation for something to happen. An online biblical lexicon lists confident expectations for God to fulfill promises. I'm ashamed to admit the truth, but I have hoped in people, products, and services prior to Christ. The Apostle Paul revealed a rich message of hope to Gentiles.

God chose Paul to relay the gospel of Jesus to Gentiles, kings, and the children of Israel, according to Acts 9. A fellow servant named Epaphroditus (Epaphras) evangelized a group of Christians in Colossae. False teachers interjected themselves. Epaphras consulted Paul, who wrote a letter from a Roman prison. He encouraged the Colossians in their faith and warned them against heretical teaching. The apostle took time in verse 25 to share by whose authority and in what capacity he, a man in prison whom they'd never met, would dare exhort the church. "I'm a servant of God and steward of His Word sent to reveal a hidden truth concealed since before the world began. Saints, God sent me to reveal Christ is your hope of glory." Gentile and Jewish believers in Jesus were preordained before generations began to receive the righteousness of God and eternal residence in heaven. Remember God's promise in Genesis that Abraham would be hailed as the father of many nations? Those many nations of every race have confessed Jesus the Hope of Glory as their Lord and Savior.

My Dad used to sing a song in church about the importance of salvation. One verse highlighted things people hoped and trusted in, instead of the Lord. Material possessions, status, and financial gain topped the list. I've built my hope on Jesus Christ. Find a quiet spot and time to self-evaluate where your hope lies. Pull out your checkbook and calendar. Where you've spent the most time and money might mean your priorities rate high there. Look up references to hope in the Bible. Read the word in context of that chapter. Journal what you learn.

Prayer: *Hope of Glory, thank You for making eternity in Heaven more than hope. Amen.*

---

[2] hope noun - Definition, pictures, pronunciation and usage notes | Oxford Advanced American Dictionary at OxfordLearnersDictionaries.com

Jesus Is — The Hope of Glory
Worksheet

To them God has chosen to make known among the Gentiles the glorious riches of this mystery, which is Christ in you, the hope of glory. (Col. 1:27)

1. In what have you placed your hope?

2. What does it mean to you to receive the Hope of Glory?

3. Use letters of the word *hope* to write blessings from the Hope of Glory.

H=

O=

P=

E=

Additional Scriptures
… being confident of this, that he who began a good work in you will carry it on to completion until the day of Christ Jesus. (Phil. 1:6)

JESUS IS — THE LAMB OF GOD

The next day, John saw Jesus coming toward him and said, "Look, the Lamb of God, who takes away the sin of the world!" (Jn. 1:29)

A nine-year-old named Mary from Massachusetts happened upon a newborn lamb whose mother had abandoned the fellow. Mary begged her father for permission to care for the lamb. She nursed it back to health; the animal followed Mary wherever she went. John Roulstone, a fellow classmate, drafted a poem about the lamb when he followed Mary to school one day. Another Mary, centuries before, gave birth to the Lamb of God, who came to take away the world's sins. He, too, follows us everywhere we go.

The annual Passover Feast instituted by God served as a reminder of Israel's deliverance from Egyptian bondage. The death angel passed over every house whose doorpost bore the blood of an unblemished lamb. This lamb foreshadowed a greater deliverance from the bondage of sin for Jews and Gentiles by Jesus, the sinless Lamb of God.

John the Baptist baptized people who repented of their sins with water in Bethabara, beyond the Jordan. Pharisees sent priests and Levites to question John's identity. He replied, "But after me comes one who is more powerful than I, whose sandals I am not worthy to carry. He will baptize you with the Holy Spirit and fire" (Mt. 3:11).

Instead of stating a formal name, the prophet emphasized his message, "In the wilderness prepare the way for the LORD" (Is. 40:3).

The next day, John viewed Jesus walking toward him and declared, "Behold the Lamb of God which takes away the sin of the world." How did he recognize his first cousin as the Messiah and sacrificial Lamb? God sent a sign: "Upon whom you see the Spirit come down and remain, the same baptizes with the Holy Spirit." John witnessed the Spirit descending from heaven like a dove, which rested on Jesus.

Roulstone's poem developed into a beloved children's song after writer Sarah Josepha Hale added more stanzas in 1830. One line asks a question we might ask about our Lamb. "Why does the lamb love Mary so?" Jesus loves us when we don't like ourselves. Like young Mary's pet, He never leaves nor forsakes and follows our every move. Let's show our appreciation to Jesus by volunteering at an animal shelter, a senior citizen's center, or library, and exhibiting warmth and affection. Pray for children and adults wounded by abandonment issues. Ask the Lord to use you as a minister of grace and encouragement.

Prayer: Thank You, Lamb of God, for shedding Your blood on Calvary. Amen.

Jesus Is — The Lamb of God
Worksheet

The next day, John saw Jesus coming toward him and said, "Look, the Lamb of God, who takes away the sin of the world!" (Jn. 1:29)

1. Who was John the Baptist?

2. Why was Jesus referred to as the Lamb of God?

3. When have you sacrificed for someone? Describe the situation, results, and reaction of the person who benefited.

Additional Scriptures

And walk in the way of love, just as Christ loved us and gave himself up for us as a fragrant offering and sacrifice to God. (Eph. 5:2)

JESUS IS—OUR FRIEND

I no longer call you servants, because a servant does not know his master's business. Instead, I have called you friends, for everything that I learned from my Father, I have made known to you. (Jn. 15:15)

A line from a popular movie cited friends as the ones who hang with and support you through the unknown. An online dictionary[3] defines a friend as someone with whom you share a bond of mutual affection. I desire to be a friend like Jesus.

Camaraderie between Christ and twelve men He'd chosen to mentor and do life with afforded them a status change from servants to friends. They shared meals, traveled together, stood up for right and against wrong, witnessed one another's vulnerabilities without judgment, yet voiced hard truths in love. Doing life together with Jesus and one another taught the disciples first-hand knowledge of loyal friendship. Through the Lord's patient teaching and loving example, they learned how to overcome negative emotions such as anger, frustration, and fear. The men were privy to one another's reactions in the worst and best of times. I believe this solidified their bond. The learners let Jesus down on more than one occasion. One of them, Judas Iscariot, took the tempter's trap and traipsed off to betray Him. Christ still referred to the remaining eleven as friends. Why? A true friend loves at all times. They'd shared an up-close, personal journey, and Jesus imparted all the information He'd received from the Father to His close companions.

Friendships flourish when nourished with love, loyalty, and respect. Jesus described love as a life of putting others first. The disciples were urged to obey Christ's commands to love as He loved as a condition of His friendship.

Research work for this devotional drew me to an alarming epiphany. My role as a friend didn't measure up in the mirror of the Word. Sure, I loved and prayed for my friends. Did I intentionally listen to and put their concerns and needs before mine? That's what Jesus did. He encouraged those near and dear to live the same life of self-sacrifice. A healthy friendship reduces stress, adds emotional support, which improves mental and physical well-being, and grants a confidante and traveling companion. Genuine friendships symbolize how Christians are chosen, redeemed by Jesus, and adopted into God's family. We select our friends based on that mutual affection mentioned at the beginning. Our ideas and opinions may not always agree, but love abounds. Wouldn't the world be sweeter if every believer were a friend like Jesus?

Prayer: Jesus, I floundered in the friendship area. Help me be more like You and less like me. Amen.

Additional Scriptures
Anyone who withholds kindness from a friend forsakes the fear of the Almighty. (Job 6:14)

A friend loves at all times, and a brother is born for a time of adversity. (Pr. 17:17)

---

[3] https://www.askdifference.com/friend-vs-companion/

Jesus Is — Our Friend
Worksheet

I no longer call you servants because a servant does not know his master's business. Instead, I have called you friends, for everything that I have learned from my Father, I have made known to you. (Jn. 15:15)

1. List three people who might name you as a good friend.

2. What's the difference between a friend and an acquaintance to you? Are you striving to be a better friend?

3. Draw a circle like a clock face and large enough to write inside. At 12:00, 3:00, 6:00, and 9:00 hours, name someone you consider part of your close set of friends. (Don't worry if there is no name for each hour.) Pray for the ones you specified at the listed hour.

Additional Scriptures
One who has unreliable friends soon comes to ruin, but there is a friend who sticks closer than a brother. (Pr. 18:24)

JESUS IS — THE LIGHT OF THE WORLD

"You are the light of the world. A town built on a hill cannot be hidden. (Mt. 5:14)

We passed mile after mile of dense mountain range and homes obscured by night's darkness, with occasional crops of illumination from twenty-four-hour diners and convenience stores. Then, up ahead, it seemed lots of lights twinkled and beckoned white-bright. Set high above the freeway, the city provided a fabulous view near and far. No wonder Jesus taught that a city set on a hill can't be hidden.

On a mountainside and before a crowd, Jesus taught the first disciples how to draw people from darkness to light and from the power of Satan to God. He taught them to beam their light brightly, so they projected near and far like a city set on a hill. Imagine how light chases away the dark of any room with the flick of a power switch and how the sun's rays chase away black, brooding clouds. Like the earlier followers of Jesus, believers bear responsibility to symbolize a sky-high city and beam the light of the gospel in actions and words. We're commissioned to spread the good news to all nations, thereby pushing back the darkness of Satan and his evil workers.

Well past the panorama we viewed during our trip, its pleasant effect still created a sense of security. Do my daily interactions with others leave a sweet scent and the dazzling light of the Savior's love? What about yours?

Here are some steps to stay lit for the Lord: Start each day with an attitude of gratitude. Remember the mission. Ask the Holy Spirit for guidance, and dress in the whole armor of God. We are the light of this world. It's time to shine, shine.

Prayer: *Light of the world, You came down to dispel darkness. May I labor as a vessel of love and shine. Amen.*

Jesus Is—The Light of The World
Worksheet

"You are the light of the world. A town built on a hill cannot be hidden. (Mt. 5:14)

1. What actions or words have dimmed your light of testimony?

2. In your words, describe what the word *light* represents.

3. List areas of darkness in our world today.

4. Who has been a bright light of Jesus' love in your life?

Additional Scriptures
While I am in the world, I am the light of the world. (Jn. 9:5)

JESUS IS — THE GOOD NEWS

"Therefore, go and make disciples of all nations, baptizing them in the name of the Father and of the Son and of the Holy Spirit..." (Mt. 28:19)

Little Emory dashed in and grabbed a glazed donut in one hand and a chocolate-covered donut in the other. Before anyone sitting inside the choir room/Sunday School classroom could scarcely utter a word, she turned and skipped out, chomping on her bounty. Moments later, the petite girl returned with five other children trailing behind her. Emory pointed to the table and grinned as her friends picked the boxes clean. She'd found something good and shared it with others.

A turbulent earthquake rocked the world. It was the first day of the week, after the Sabbath. The earthquake's potent force heralded an angel from heaven to roll away the stone. He brought glad tidings to Mary Magdalene and the other Mary, saying, "He is not here; he has risen, just as he said. Come and see the place where he lay." (Mt. 28:6).

Somewhat afraid, yet filled with joy, the women rushed to report their empty tomb encounter with the disciples. Out of nowhere, the risen Savior intercepted them. "Greetings. Don't be afraid. Go and tell my brothers that I'll meet them in Galilee." Once again, the ladies were commissioned with a message and a measure of reassurance.

The eleven followers listened to the women's remarkable news and remembered Jesus' directions prior to His crucifixion. They traveled to a mountain in Galilee, and He met them there. Reactions were mixed. Almost all worshipped the Messiah, but Thomas doubted. Christ showed him the nail scars to prove His identity. The disciples were charged with carrying on the mission for which they'd trained for the last three years. "All authority in heaven and on earth has been given to me. Therefore, go and make disciples of all nations, baptizing them in the name of the Father and of the Son and of the Holy Spirit" (Mt. 28:18-19).

Jesus said — No more prejudice against the Gentiles. Christ suffered and sacrificed so that *all* might come to salvation through belief in who He is. Our witness must encompass the world at large, not pick and choose. Making disciples means helping someone learn to follow Christ in day-by-day actions, speech, and thoughts. Baptizing in the Holy Trinity shows a public profession of faith. The Lord pledged never to leave those first disciples alone. His promise remains true for each ambassador today.

I marveled at a child's innocent and practical demonstration of sharing something good. Adults and youth appreciated a quick snack during Sunday School connection or before morning worship. Emory could have discovered the treats, eaten her fill, and not told anyone. Instead, the petite cutie skipped down the hall and guided back five more kids. I imagined the initial reactions of the little ones she told.

Retain a child-like faith to share the gospel with as many people as possible. Look for unusual places and ways, such as sharing an inspiring verse on your restaurant receipt or in conversations about the day, whether a praise or need for prayer. Remember, sharing the good news is as easy as sharing a donut. Jesus is the Good News.

Prayer: Lord, thank You for rising from a borrowed tomb and being our Good News. Amen.

Jesus Is— The Good News
Worksheet

Therefore, go and make disciples of all nations, baptizing them in the name of the Father and of the Son and of the Holy Spirit. (Mt. 28:19)

1. Define a disciple in your words.

2. Are you a disciple of Christ?

3. Describe how you have previously or plan to go and make disciples.

4. What does "baptize in the name of the Father, Son, and Holy Spirit" mean?

Additional Scriptures
And the things you have heard me say in the presence of many witnesses entrust to reliable people who will also be qualified to teach others. (2 Tim. 2:2)

JESUS IS — THE BLESSED GIVER

In everything I did, I showed you that by this kind of hard work we must help the weak, remembering the words the Lord Jesus himself said: 'It is more blessed to give than to receive.' (Acts 20:35)

Ten-year-old Elena donated her birthday money to help purchase water for fire victims. Martha sought prayer via our church messenger thread for sick members and preteens at camp. Someone else mentioned those on a foreign mission trip and the bereaved. Each of these examples compelled fervent prayer and inspired an excited desire to give. A warmth of contentment washed away fraught self-concerns as my focus shifted to those in need. Ages ago, the Apostle Paul discovered that the blessing of giving far outweighs receiving.

The Apostle Paul greeted, mentored, and exchanged goodbyes with all kinds of people in his lifetime. Acts 20 records Paul's farewell encouragement to the Ephesian Elders, whom he would never see again. Near the end of the chapter, he sums up with a quote from Jesus. "It is more blessed to give than to receive" (Acts 20:35).

What last words would you say to loved ones? The men met Paul at Miletus so he would not be delayed for Pentecost in Jerusalem. I hope they greeted and asked after one another's well-being before the business. Luke left that to our divine imagination. Paul's speech started when the elders got there.

"You know how I lived the whole time I was with you, from the first day I came into the province of Asia. I served the Lord with great humility and with tears and amid severe testing by the plots of my Jewish opponents. You know that I have not hesitated to preach anything that would be helpful to you but have taught you publicly and from house to house. I have declared to both Jews and Greeks that they must turn to God in repentance and have faith in our Lord Jesus. Keep watch over yourselves and all the flock of which the Holy Spirit has made you overseers. So be on your guard!" (Acts 20:18-21, 28).

Paul invoked God's blessings on the elders and shared a lesson on working and helping others. "You yourselves know that these hands of mine have supplied for the needs of me and my companions. In everything I did, I showed you that by this kind of hard work we must help the weak, remembering the words the Lord Jesus himself said: 'It is more blessed to give than to receive'" (Acts 20:35-36).

Thanksgiving, Christmas, and Easter represent my three favorite holidays because they inspire giving. Gifts of your presence and sincere prayers keep going and might please any age. God designed us to long for fellowship with one another and petition on behalf of others. Let's ask the Lord to beam a light on those in our schools, at our jobs, in our church, or neighborhood whom we might encourage. Create a special "Just Because I Care" day to cheer a child or adult. Send notes of appreciation to trash and street crews. Practice giving of your time, talent, and service without expecting anything back. Be like Jesus.

Prayer: Lord, may I give from a pure heart without expecting or wanting payback, but because of how good You are to me. Amen.

Jesus Is— The Blessed Giver
Worksheet

In everything I did, I showed you that by this kind of hard work we must help the weak, remembering the words the Lord Jesus himself said: "It is more blessed to give than to receive." (Acts 20:35)

1. What did Paul mean by "In everything I did" in the verse above?

2. Have you offered a gift to another with impure motives? Why? What were the results?

3. Have you sacrificed and given freely to one in desperate need? What prompted your actions?

4. Would you rather receive or give a gift?

Additional Scriptures
… And walk in the way of love, just as Christ loved us and gave himself up for us as a fragrant offering and sacrifice to God. (Eph. 5:2)

JESUS IS — THE GREAT PHYSICIAN

Jesus reached out his hand and touched the man. "I am willing," he said. "Be clean!" Immediately, he was cleansed of his leprosy. (Mt. 8:3)

A horrible pain cinched my neck and head in an unyielding vise. I searched for an internal medicine physician who might have an appointment available. One unsuccessful call after another increased frustration but yielded no result. A song on a Christian radio station reminded me that Christ is our all and prompted me to stop and pray. "Lord, help. Forgive me for not asking You, the Great Physician. According to Your will, please heal my head — release pain's bridle."

Jesus cured every disease among the people in Galilee. Multitudes followed Him. It's important to interject that Jesus viewed the crowds through a lens of compassion and love as scattered sheep without a shepherd. He completed His longest sermon ever and descended from the mountain. Among a throng trailing behind Him stepped a leper, whose quest for restoration compelled him to defy Levitical laws on uncleanness. (Lev. 13 and 14)

The leper bowed in humble reverence. This action expressed an undiluted faith in Jesus' sovereign power to heal. "Lord, if it is Thy will, You can make me clean," further demonstrated the leper's meek appeal, not assumption, that the Lord should help. The Great Physician reached out and touched the unclean man. Right away, his leprosy cleared.

Jesus answered my prayer. Severe hurt relaxed its grip and released my head and neck. "Thank You, Great Physician." The Lord ordained doctors and medicines, yet we must remember He is the Source. Our first call should go to the One who is always accessible, requires no insurance, and shed blood to pay our bill centuries ago. The Great Physician makes house calls.

Prayer: Thank You, Great Physician, for heeding our cries and healing our wounds. Amen.

Additional Scriptures
At sunset, the people brought to Jesus all who had various kinds of sickness, and laying his hands on each one, he healed them. (Lk. 4:40)

Jesus Is — The Great Physician
Worksheet

Jesus reached out his hand and touched the man. "I am willing," he said. "Be clean!" Immediately, he was cleansed of his leprosy. (Mt. 8:3)

1. Describe your impression of Jesus as the Great Physician.

2. List areas where you, a family member, or a friend could use the Healer's touch.

3. Have you ever felt unclean in your thoughts and actions?

4. Besides physical, what other types of healing might you expect from the Great Physician?

Additional Scriptures
On hearing this, Jesus said, "It is not the healthy who need a doctor, but the sick. (Mt. 9:12)

JESUS IS — THE ONE WE SHOULD OBEY

His mother said to the servants, "Do whatever he tells you." (Jn. 2:5)

Kelsey loved her soft pink rug. "Vacuum it every day, like the label says, and it will last longer," her mom advised. Instead, she swept it with a broom. On the surface, it appeared dirt-free, but the broom bristles buried debris deeper into the fibers. Failure to follow proper care instructions can shorten the lifespan and devalue, while adhering to maintenance labels assures optimum use and longevity. Likewise, Christians live their best lives when they follow their Manufacturer's (Jesus') directions.

The wine jars ran dry at a marriage celebration in Cana, Galilee. Jesus, the disciples, and His mother, Mary, were guests. Perhaps Mary aimed to alleviate two pressing problems with one solution: her Son, the Savior. Picture the mother strolling up beside Him and whispering, "They have no more wine," and hoping He would say, "I got this, Mom." She wanted a public display of His power. I wonder what our fully human, divine Savior's facial expression was at the announcement and His mother's expectant gaze? He addressed her in a term of endearment, 'Woman,' and asserted firm yet gentle control. Even though Jesus refused the public show, Mary instructed the servers, "Do whatever He tells you." When the servers followed Christ's instructions, six jars of water transformed into choice wine.

The morning after Kelsey declined to use a vacuum, her Bible app verse came from Colossians 3. Immediately, her mom's words about following instructions popped into mind. Kelsey decided to vacuum. She delighted in the noticeable difference because she'd adhered to the manufacturer's label and obeyed her mom. Obedience rewards. Failure to comply costs. Lean not to your understanding. Study God's Word and follow the Creator's instructions to live your best life.

Prayer: Jesus, Son of God, bless us to hear, understand, and abide by what You tell us to do. Amen.

Jesus Is—The One We Should Obey
Worksheet

His mother said to the servants, "Do whatever he tells you." (Jn. 2:5)

1. Name the most recent person you were commanded to obey.

2. List some rewards of wholehearted obedience to Jesus.

3. When have you chosen to do what your flesh and the enemy whispered instead of listening to the Lord? What were the results? Have you made any adjustments?

Additional Scriptures
Jesus said, "If you hold to my teaching, you are really my disciples. (Jn. 8:31b)

1. In what area of your life are you not doing what Jesus told you to do?

2. What life debris are you sweeping over and burying deeper?

3. What's one step you can take today to begin a deep cleaning?

4. Mary wanted people to see Jesus's power. How can the world view Jesus through you?

Additional Scriptures
Very truly I tell you, whoever believes in me will do the works I have been doing. (Jn. 14:12a)

JESUS IS — SHEPHERD OF BELOVED, NOT BLACK SHEEP

"I am the good shepherd. The good shepherd lays down his life for the sheep. (Jn. 10:11)

The sign on the approaching vehicle read, "I'm the black jeep of the family." How cute. I used to feel like the black sheep of *my* family because my business college degree didn't come from a four-year university, nor did I have the perfect marriage. I judged my worthiness based on others' opinions of me. My whole co-dependent outlook changed once I met the Good Shepherd.

In some regions, sheep farmers placed their herds together in one fenced-in area called a fold. Sheep recognized the voice of their shepherd and followed when he called them by name. Good shepherds fed their beloved flocks even when winter and fall made pasture grass scarce. They often slept near the fold to protect the sheep from thieves and wild animals. Quick running water frightened sheep, so shepherds searched for still pools to water them. David, a shepherd boy, penned Psalm 23. His time spent caring for and loving sheep that depended on him for direction, protection, and provision compelled David to acknowledge God as the Good Shepherd of His beloved sheep. He envisioned goodness and mercy pursuing beloved sheep all the days of their lives, so no good thing did they lack. Because the sheep obey their Shepherd, they no longer live in a temporary fold but dwell in the house of the LORD forever.

Wikipedia[4] defines *black sheep* as a negative term used in the English language to define a family member who doesn't fit in. It originated from the rare sheep born with black wool that proved difficult to dye. Think about what believers are called to be: We should stand apart from the world and not be tossed to and fro by all the false doctrines. A black sheep could translate into a valuable, beloved sheep. Let's spread the word. Pray for unbelievers (lost sheep). Be ready to answer the hope that wells within you. Follow in faith. Don't turn back. In the Good Shepherd's family, there are no outcasts. All are beloved.

Prayer: *Good Shepherd, where You lead, I will follow. Amen.*

Reflect: *Have you viewed yourself or someone else as the black sheep? Take another look through the lenses of God's love and grace.*

---

[4] Black sheep - Wikipedia

Jesus Is—Shepherd of Beloved, Not Black Sheep
Worksheet

"I am the good shepherd. The good shepherd lays down his life for the sheep. (Jn. 10:11)

1. Define the word *good* in the verse above.

2. How would you describe a black sheep?

3. What does *beloved* mean? Describe what it means to you to be a beloved follower of Jesus.

Additional Scriptures
The Lord is my shepherd; I lack nothing. (Ps. 23:1)

JESUS IS—THE BURDEN BEARER

Come to me, all you who are weary and burdened, and I will give you rest. (Mt. 11:28)

A loud thwack against the front of the house shot shivers of dread down my spine. I rushed to discover its source and gasped at the sight of my full-view storm door ripped from the hinges. Material and contractor prices have skyrocketed in the last three years. I still pondered how to pay for a new door when high winds struck again, one week later, and ripped off a wooden gate from the backyard.

"What's next?" I voiced concern to a friend. "My budget is already stretched to the max." Widows craved home repairs about like the Israelites cringed at foreign oppression and human religious burden. The less needed, the better our temperament. Jesus invited those heavy laden to His light burden and easy yoke.

Jesus invited all who *labored* (physical or mental exertion placed on oneself) and were heavy *laden* (burdened or weighed down by others) to come to Him and receive rest. This serene peace appealed to the Israelites, who sought a simple life without the oppressive Roman rule and long list of growing traditions imposed by local Pharisees and religious rulers. They were yoked, enslaved. Jesus offered an easy yoke and a lighter burden. Farmers of the past used a Y-shaped instrument to bind an older, more experienced ox to a young or new one. The stronger one bore the burden and guided the younger animal as it learned the process. The Lord offered to link Himself beside us—to teach and guide. He bears our burdens. Our way seems clear once we've learned the Lord's character and adopted His perspective. Yoked alongside Jesus, believers participate in a disciple relationship with our burden bearer.

The shattered storm door and crushed front gate caused me to reflect on my brokenness and desire to live in peace, purposed like Christ. We can yoke ourselves up to needless worries instead of casting all our cares on the Lord. Remember whose and who you are. Trials will come. Things will fall apart, but we don't have to put them back together alone. The Burden Bearer watches. He's ever near.

Prayer: Lord, thank You for yoking me with You and showing me what to do. Amen.

Jesus Is—The Burden Bearer
Worksheet

"Come to me, all you who are weary and burdened, and I will give you rest. (Mt. 11:28)

1. When was the last time you felt weary? Burdened?

a. Where did you go?

b. How did you obtain relief?

2. List three examples of each physical and spiritual burden that may concern you.

3. Define *rest* in your words.

Additional Scriptures
Surely, he took up our pain and bore our suffering… (Is. 53:4a)

The Best Gift — A Poem by SD Simms

I offer the best gift that doesn't belong to me.
'Tis the good news of Jesus and what happened at Calvary.
He descended from heaven to be crucified and buried.
Three days later, the Lord rose from a borrowed tomb.
All Power of heaven and earth is in His hand.
God's Son is the mystery and original plan.
Everyone, Jew *and* Gentile, can be saved.
Believe in your heart in who Jesus is and confess with your mouth.
The Holy Spirit immediately seals you until the day of redemption.
Study the word, pray, and worship in truth.
Be prepared for the enemy to cause trouble and attempt to steal your gumption.
Remember, don't fear. Christ warned there would be days like this.
Study the word, trust, and obey.
This world, a foreign land, won't always stay.
Believers are blessed by God's gift. We're bound for our permanent home in Paradise, one day.

For God so loved the world that he gave his one and only son, that whoever believes in him shall not perish but have eternal life. (Jn. 3:16)

JESUS IS—THE TRANSFORMER

Therefore, if anyone is in Christ, the new creation has come: The old has gone, the new is here! (2 Cor. 5:17)

TV commercials promote new and improved products that manufacturers have repackaged to make them more eye-catching. Ads claim the revamped merchandise works better than the original version. The Apostle Paul told the Corinthians that those who are in Christ are new creations.

Inner renewal does not occur because one transforms his or her outer appearance. The outside of a house may gleam with a fresh paint job and a recent roof, but inside remain the same tired, broken-down walls and trash-filled floors behind a state-of-the-art entry door. That house symbolizes our broken spiritual condition until we seek an inner heart change. Unforgiveness binds, hatred heats prejudice, and resentment trumps rest and peace, but an emergency visit with the Transformer alters our attitude and character. Studying and meditating on the Word promotes an actual heart change. The old passes away. Christ renews.

Two orange juice containers read "New and Improved." The first name brand tastes the same, but it's two ounces less in quantity and has a slimmer design. An inner change shines through to the outside. People notice negative words missing from your speech and wonder at your calm demeanor. Determine to start and end each day as Christ's representative. Memorize scripture that resonates to encourage and motivate yourself and others. When you fail, confess, and start over. The Transformer cleans and forgives.

Prayer: Thank You, Lord, for transforming us into new and better beings focused on loving and honoring in living and serving. Amen

Jesus Is—The Transformer
Worksheet

Therefore, if anyone is in Christ, the new creation has come: The old has gone, the new is here! (2 Cor. 5:17)

1. What promises can you claim about this verse?

2. List some scripture verses to study and further enforce these promises.

3. Who led you to Christ? Is your transformation noticeable? How can it gleam?

4. Why is being a new creation vital to you?

5. Where did God illustrate ashes transformed into beauty today?

6. What concerns burden you? Transform them from stones of worry to pebbles of peace as you pass them from your bag to His.

Additional Scriptures
Do not conform to the pattern of this world but be transformed by the renewing of your mind. Then you will be able to test and approve what God's will is — his good, pleasing and perfect will. (Rom. 12:2)

JESUS IS — THE NEVER-ENDING STORY

Jesus did not let him, but said, "Go home to your own people and tell them how much the Lord has done for you, and how he has had mercy on you." (Mk. 5:19)

Storytelling is a passion, whether in written form or expressed orally. Every person has a story of who, why, how, when, and where. It's called life. Recollections of childhood memories, sweet romances, and heart-drumming suspense rank high on my book list. My favorite, by far, is the never-ending story of Jesus in the Bible. The imagery used by our Creator to describe His ancestors and their stiff-necked disobedience is rich and real. The immaculate conception and subsequent birth of a baby boy to a young Jewish virgin led to miraculous healings and wise teachings by our fully human, fully divine Savior.

In the beginning, Jesus and the Father created man with a soul, designed to long for fellowship and love with Them and one another. At the end of my earthly life, Jesus will transport me to His eternal home. Did you know you're an important character in Jesus' story? Which chapter of life are you in now?

Is it in the chapter of decisions where He seeks an invitation to your heart (Rev. 3:20)?

Perhaps a Psalm of praise for a season of celebrations (Ps. 100)?

Have family issues, financial strain, or illness burdened and distressed you? Did you petition the One who can give you rest (Mk. 7:32)?

Wherever you're stationed in life, the Hero remains the same, yesterday, today, and forevermore. Christ is the never-ending story.

Prayer: Jesus, Author and Finisher of each story, help me to follow Your table of contents for each chapter of my life. Amen.

Reflect: With whom can I share the story of Jesus today? This week?

Jesus Is—The Never-ending Story
Worksheet

Jesus did not let him, but said, "Go home to your own people and tell them how much the Lord has done for you, and how he has had mercy on you." (Mk. 5:19)

1. What images do the words *never-ending* bring to your mind?

2. What's your favorite Bible story? Why?

3. What chapter of your life story are you living? Have you written (invited) the Hero (Jesus) to take part? If so, what role will Jesus have?

Additional Scriptures
When they had seen him, they spread the word concerning what had been told them about this child. (Lk. 2:17)

JESUS IS— THE ONE TO KNOW HIS POWER AND SUFFERING

I want to know Christ—yes, to know the power of his resurrection and participation in his sufferings, becoming like him in his death. (Phil. 3:10)

Two years ago, I asked Jesus to teach me to love like He loves. Why did I not consider the cost? The gospels of Matthew, Mark, Luke, and John record *their* journeys with Christ, each in their own words. The Lord crossed racial barriers, touched the dead and defiled, and ate with tax collectors. In return, townspeople ridiculed and mocked Him. Priests and law experts stalked Him, and His family rejected Him. Jesus continued to serve. That's my goal.

Paul described his quest in living like Christ as "pressing toward the mark…" (Phil. 3:14).

The apostle understood that before he could follow Jesus' example, he needed to know Him deeper. Paul longed for a best friend kind of fellowship with the Lord. He would celebrate the joys and miracles and embrace pain and suffering. The apostle's mission as a light to the Gentiles earned him whippings, beatings with rods, a stoning, being shipwrecked, and experiencing danger everywhere he traveled from robbers and amongst his people. Yet, Paul endured all hardships as temporary tests on the journey to glory for God.

Family estrangement, rejection, and misunderstanding have plagued my journey. All three combined don't fill a teaspoon compared to what our Savior endured on the cross (Heb. 12:4). No, we're not Jesus, but we have the same Father. The Lord asked for power to accomplish His goals. The Holy Spirit, the same power that raised *Jesus* from the dead, rests in every believer.

The Lord hears and answers our prayers, and I'm convinced He has a delightful sense of humor. He placed me in situations and with people who tested the depths of unconditional love. It's never convenient, quite often sacrificial and messy, yet soul-stirring, satisfying, and transforming to know an nth of Christ's suffering and love for humanity.

Seek His help. Have a made-up mind to be a faithful follower. Offer the same grace you're gifted to the difficult. Finally, love, whether it's returned or not. Remember the price Christ suffered that we may know eternal love.

Prayer: Teach me, Lord, teach me. My heart is willing — the flesh rebels.
Amen.

Reflect: The road to heaven is narrow with few travelers because of all the trials, flat tires, wrong ways, detours, and potholes of traveled life.

Jesus Is—The One to Know His Power and Suffering Worksheet

I want to know Christ—yes, to know the power of his resurrection and participation in his sufferings, becoming like him in his death. (Phil. 3:10)

1. Name a friend whom you consider a close confidante. List three reasons why you chose this friend.

2. What joyful occasions have you celebrated together? When have you supported one another during a time of crisis?

3. Describe what it means to know Christ's power and fellowship in His sufferings.

Additional Scriptures
Therefore, since Christ suffered in his body, arm yourselves also with the same attitude, because whoever suffers in the body is done with sin. (1 Pet. 4:1)

JESUS IS—THE ROCK TO CLING TO IN AN UNEXPECTED FLOOD

The rain came down, the streams rose, and the winds blew and beat against that house; yet it did not fall, because it had its foundation on the rock. (Mt. 7:25)

Tuesday morning started ahead of schedule. I washed C-pap tubing and mask while waiting for my daily video vlog to post. A few minutes later, I stepped back into the bedroom to check the uploading process. My phone rang. A conversation ensued. A splashing noise caught my attention. *Oh no! I left the water running.* The C-Pap supplies bobbed under the faucet like rubber ducklings floating near a river fall. Imagine *my* expression while watching water spill over and spread across new flooring and base moulding. I lunged for the lever and slammed the faucet off while snatching towels to staunch the flood. Praises and thanks swirled in my heart and circulated in a grateful cadence like my feet swirled soppy towels about the floor. *God* knew *this would happen. He had blessed me to purchase waterproof floors.* I grinned. This house and the one that encased my soul were built on firm foundations—the first of long-lasting resources and the latter on Jesus Christ.

Jesus chose elements of nature and homebuilders in the last seven verses of the Sermon on the Mount. The section illustrated how believers should listen and obey instructions. Therefore, the first word in verse 24 pointed back to all the Lord had taught thus far and led into the next objective. A wise builder built his house on solid rock. Neither gale-force winds nor rigorous rainstorms destroyed the house, which stood on a sure foundation. Along came a foolish contractor who constructed his home on sand. Rain swept down and flooded the area. Winds whipped and blew until the dwelling fell. Both men worked hard to build, but the unwise one did not start with a proper foundation. The job required a solid, immovable material like rock, but he chose sand. The sand represented man's opinions. Jesus Christ reigns as the unchangeable second person of the Holy Trinity. Our faith should be built upon no other foundation than Jesus.

Trials transpire as suddenly as my unexpected bathroom accident. Storms of loss due to death, financial distress, or relational issues may flood in like fierce winds, bringing pelting rain and white-hot lightning. Choose to lean and depend on our sure foundation of Jesus. Keep an arsenal of *emergency* scriptures memorized to encourage yourself and others. Seek God's guidance for a prayer partner to pray together in faith.

Prayer: When the storms of life rage, help me remember to cling to You, Lord.

Reflect: I'm thankful for spiritual growth. I may stagger and sway in the storms until I kneel to pray.

Jesus Is—The Rock to Cling to In an Unexpected Flood
Worksheet

The rain came down, the streams rose, and the winds blew and beat against that house; yet it did not fall, because it had its foundation on the rock. (Mt. 7:25)

1. List three different types of storms you have survived. What did it take to overcome?

2. What are the characteristics of a rock that you would associate with Jesus?

3. What consequences have you faced for listening to your own or another person's opinion instead of seeking guidance from the Lord?

Additional Scriptures
Do not merely listen to the word and so deceive yourselves. Do what it says. (Jms. 1:22 NIV)

JESUS IS — THE WAY MAKER

... by a new and living way opened for us through the curtain, that is, his body ... (Heb. 10:20)

Fifteen minutes before a normal alarm time, I woke up eager to talk to God and start a new day. It's a precious privilege to worship and pray in public without fear of severe persecution. Centuries ago, God's people depended on a priest, chosen by lot, to enter the Holy of Holies section of the temple and pray for them. I'm thankful Jesus made a way for believers to approach God's throne and petition for ourselves.

God chose Aaron (Moses' older brother) and his sons from the tribe of Levi to serve as priests and mediate between Him and the people of Israel. He instituted laws on Mt Sinai, which spelled out the Levites' responsibilities of offering sacrifices, and how to approach the tabernacle. Holy God expected the priests to prepare both body and mind to talk to Him. They sacrificed a sin offering for themselves, symbolizing a need for pardon for past guilt—a burnt offering dedicated the men wholeheartedly to God.

Aaron held the office of high priest. The high priest was the only one allowed to go past the curtain into the Holy of Holies, where the Ark of the Testimony rested. The Ark represented the very presence of God. Once a year, the great high priest went in to offer sacrifices for the people and himself. Part of the priest's formal attire included the breastplate of judgment. Twelve stone jewels, each a different color for the twelve tribes of Israel, were inlaid on the front of the breastplate, and a small pouch inserted above the heart held divine casting lots called *Urim*, the first letter of the Hebrew alphabet, and *Thummim*, the last letter of the Hebrew alphabet.

All priests were Levites, but not all Levites held office as priests. God expected priests to uphold high moral and spiritual integrity and pure hearts. Two of Aaron's sons were destroyed by fire for flagrant disobedience. Others took care of the tabernacle maintenance and furnishings. The Levitical priest and the law were not created for permanent use. Despite yearly sacrifices and awareness of God's commands, Israel and Judah disobeyed, served idols, and profaned God's name. The priests hoped to instill obedience and perfection in the people, but they, too, were sinners. Christ's death ended the era of the Levitical priesthood and the Old Covenant. God placed His Word in men's hearts and promised a new covenant. Jesus Christ, the Great High Priest of the New Covenant, came from the tribe of Judah and was a priest after the order of Melchizedek.

Who is *Melchizedek* (righteous king)? Genesis 14 identified him as priest of the Most-High God and King of Salem (Salem means peace), whose parentage, birth, and death dates are not recorded. Melchizedek refreshed Abraham after a tumultuous battle and blessed him. Abraham, in turn, tithed the king like an offering dedicated to God. Melchizedek, a human king, foreshadowed our Great High Priest, Jesus, the one who made a way for perfection. He who began a good work in you will complete it to the end (Phil. 1:6).

Jesus sacrificed His life once, and that's sufficient for all the world's sin penalty. The Temple veil was torn in two. He made a way for you and me to access God's presence now and forever. He opened doors to kick out bitterness, hatred, old hurts, and habits and fill up on mercy, truth, and love. Jesus has no sins and is our advocate at the Father's right hand.

Praying and reading the Word gives me great joy. Start an ongoing list of how Jesus has made a way in your life. Encourage others with a testimony of the Lord's faithfulness. Memorize verses that remind you that Jesus is the Way Maker.

Prayer: *Jesus, thank You for taking my place on Calvary and making a way to God for me. Amen.*

Jesus Is — The Way Maker
Worksheet

... by a new and living way opened for us through the curtain, that is, his body ... (Heb. 10:20)

1. Write down the first sentence that comes to your mind when you hear *Way Maker*.

2. Who has made a way for you and how? (Give three examples)

3. Describe how *Melchizedek's* name and the meaning of *Salem* point to Jesus.

Additional Scriptures
Therefore, since we have a great high priest who has ascended into heaven, Jesus the Son of God, let us hold firmly to the faith we profess. (Heb. 4:14)

HO THEOS TES AGAPES — JESUS IS LOVE

Finally, brothers and sisters, rejoice! Strive for full restoration, encourage one another, be of one mind, live in peace. And the God of love and peace will be with you. (2 Cor. 13:11)

What images come to mind when you hear the word *love*? Do mental flashes of roses, red hearts, and kisses appear? Perhaps you envision a couple locked in a warm embrace. The American Heritage Dictionary[5] defines *love* as deep affection and strong fondness for a person, place, or thing. God's love stems from faithful commitment and sacrifice. It's called *agape* (from the Greek word Agapao).

God demonstrated His love for humanity by sending Christ to die for our sins. He commanded believers to exhibit the same affection for Him and one another. The Apostle Paul penned, "Love is kind, long-suffering, and seeks not its own," in 1 Corinthians 13, known as the chapter of love. Paul proved those words by admonishing a Corinthian assembly in love despite personal attacks on his apostolic authority. Problems akin to present-day worldliness, false teaching, and discord plagued the church founded on Paul's first visit to Corinth. The apostle hungered to transform people's perspectives and priorities to the gospel of Christ, God's greatest gift of love to the world. Chapters 10 through 13 of 2 Corinthians took on a serious tone like a parent reminding errant yet beloved children of sobering truths. Perhaps Paul leaned forward and inked each fervent word on spiritual weapons of warfare, his sufferings, and love for the church. "Farewell, brothers," he signed off. "Live in peace. The God of love shall be with you."

Do the following phrases sound familiar? "Oh, my goodness, I love that dress." "I love chocolate." Last week, Cara loved Harold. This week, she's crazy for Cody. Names and items might be different, but the misused concept remains. Societies L O V E to express temporary feelings. Action, commitment, and self-sacrifice characterize godly love.

God loves without respect for persons and regardless of reciprocation. He commands every child to follow suit. Remember the greatest commandments? Love the Lord with all your heart and your neighbor as yourself. *Neighbor* defines everyone else. Read 1 Corinthians 13 aloud for two weeks. Choose one verse each day to memorize. Make a list of those you struggle to love. Pray daily for their comfort, love, and peace in God.

Prayer: *God of love, may I illustrate You in speech and deed. Amen*

---

[5] love - definition and meaning

Jesus Is Love
Worksheet

Finally, brothers and sisters, rejoice! Strive for full restoration, encourage one another, be of one mind, live in peace. And the God of love and peace will be with you. (2 Cor. 13:11)

1. What thoughts can you ponder about God's love to exemplify it more?

2. What promises can you claim from the scripture above?

3. Define *agape* in your words.

4. Write down ways God has demonstrated His love to you.

5. What prayer can you pray for someone difficult to love?

Additional Scriptures
I want to know Christ — yes, to know the power of his resurrection and participation in his sufferings, becoming like him in his death, and so, somehow, attaining to the resurrection from the dead. (Phil. 3:10-11)

JESUS IS—THE LORD OF HOPE

Brothers and sisters, we do not want you to be uninformed about those who sleep in death, so that you do not grieve like the rest of mankind, who have no hope. (1 Thess. 4:13)

Jerry went home after church today, not the rural route location or the physical address of Hospice. Jerry graduated to heaven. He'd purposed to draw others to Christ through music until illness drained his stamina. Pain punched the pit of my stomach and heart for his wife, Carol, and teenage son, Eric. I'm grateful their grief won't be without hope. Nelson's Bible Dictionary[6] defined *hope* as a firm assurance and confident expectancy in God. Believers cling to the characteristics that set them apart from unbelievers. Hope builds remarkable strength, which helps Christians understand death as the needed route to our permanent home with Jesus. Those who die in the Lord close their eyes on earth's side of pain, sorrow, and disarray and open them in paradise with Jesus. The church at Thessalonica voiced concern about where their deceased ancestors spent eternity. The Apostle Paul gave them hope.

The city of Thessalonica claimed a fame of wealth, political autonomy, and immoral vice. Leadership problems and rejection plagued Paul's preaching of the gospel at a church that was confused about the second coming of Christ. Negative Jews and Gentiles questioned his authority and attempted to defame Paul's character. That added to the angst of people troubled by the fate of loved ones who died before the Lord returned. Paul and his companions, Silas and Timothy, enlightened the people's understanding and soothed away concern, "We've come to put your minds at ease. If you believe that Jesus died and rose again, know for sure that those who sleep in Him will be raised too. Your relatives are taking a nap. Those in Christ belong to Him, alive or dead. Belong. When it's time to call the church out of the world, Jesus will sound a loud alarm. Those asleep in Him will rise first, then we who are alive will be caught up together in the clouds to meet our Lord in the air. So shall we ever be." What splendid words of hope to comfort and encourage one another. Jesus is well able to fill us with inexpressible joy and peace if we trust and obey. Rest on the rock of His unfailing hope and love.

Jerry walked the testimony he spoke. He inspired faith, love, perseverance, and hope in all age groups at church. He lived to praise the Lord. Sometimes we struggle with knowing what to say to the grief-stricken. The thought of visiting and not knowing what to say to a bereaved family terrified me in the past. That changed when *I* lost a child. It wasn't what people *said* that touched my heart. I drew much comfort from their presence. Life involves trials and challenges. Infuse rays of hope to others by your positive presence, a warm hug, a contagious smile, or a listening ear. When attending homegoing services, pray for salvation for the unsaved in the congregation. Send a card to a co-worker, a cashier at a local store, or a student at school who has lost a family member. If they're coffee or smoothie fans, you might include a small gift card for a drink. Readers love $5.00 Amazon cards. May the eyes of their hearts be opened to the glorious hope of glory.

Prayer: Lord, thank You for being our living hope. What a day it will be to see You face to face. Amen.

---

[6] Nelson's New Illustrated Bible Dictionary. Copyright 1995, 1986 by Thomas Nelson Publishers ISBN 0-8407-2071-8 (CB)

Jesus is — The Lord of Hope
Worksheet

Brothers and sisters, we do not want you to be uninformed about those who sleep in death, so that you do not grieve like the rest of mankind, who have no hope. (1 Thess. 4:13)

1. What is the significance of Paul addressing the people as brothers and sisters?

2. What were they uninformed about?

3. Who is 'the rest of mankind?'

4. Define *hope* in this verse context?

5. From where do you glean hope?

A co-worker shares how she longs for her husband to spend more time with their family. Both have Sundays off. She and the children attend church. Lately, her spouse has planned activities that conflict with the worship time.

How would you inspire hope and encourage your co-worker?

Additional Scriptures
He will wipe every tear from their eyes. There will be no more death or mourning or crying or pain, for the old order of things has passed away. (Rev. 21:4)

JESUS IS— THE PEACE THAT SAYS, "DON'T BE ANXIOUS"

Do not be anxious about anything, but in every situation, by prayer and petition, with thanksgiving, present your requests to God. (Phil. 4:6)

One morning, I read a devotional article that suggested we should pray and connect to God with head and heart. The Word for You Today,[7] a daily devotional, stated, "It's not about an increased amount of Bible scriptures read, but an intentional listening to understand, and live out the principle." I searched for a prayer journal among a haphazard pile on a desk to record names of those who'd come to mind as I meditated on Philippians 4:6. *Do not be anxious about anything, but in every situation, by prayer and petition, with thanksgiving, present your requests to God.*

Frustration climbed like the July heat in Texas temperatures when the book remained lost. Several key things stood out in verse 5. I needed to jot them down before I forgot. Verse 6 urged prayer, and I yearned to write out my list. "Why can't I find one?" I mulled aloud into the still of pre-dawn. *Don't be anxious.* The words were voiced audibly as if someone whispered in my ear. "Huh?" Immediate peace settled my heart and mind. "Thank You, Lord," Uncovering my Bible from the tumbled desk, I picked it up to reread aloud Philippians 4:5-9.

An old church bulletin fell out. The Lord supplied a source to record needs. Paul's words encouraged his beloved converts in Philippi and freed me from frustration.

Devotionals allow us to grasp comprehension of the Word in past and present-day applications. Relatable stories reel readers toward calm, courage, and confidence through relevant scripture. Philippians 4 inspires joy despite trials and promotes a positive attitude and serene assurance of the Lord's return. Tell the Lord what you need and thank Him for what He has already done. Meditate and memorize Philippians 4:6. Invite whomever the Lord puts in your heart to study and remember the passage. Write the verse on sticky notes and place them where you will view them often. Consider sharing your testimony to introduce others to our excellent source of peace.

Prayer: *Lord, thank You for being all-powerful, everywhere, and meeting needs even before we ask. Please guide those you have ordained or allowed in positions of leadership, release the chains that bind those addicted to drugs, alcohol, pornography, or other illicit and harmful ways, comfort those burdened in sorrow and pain, and draw those close to you who have not yet believed in who You are. We trust and depend on You, our King. Amen.*

---

[7]Personal Subscription - The Word For You Today

Jesus Is—The Peace That Says, "Don't Be Anxious"
Worksheet

Do not be anxious about anything, but in every situation, by prayer and petition, with thanksgiving, present your requests to God. (Phil. 4:6)

1. Define *peace* in your words.

2. Describe a moment when you have felt anxious.

3. a. Describe an answered prayer of *yes* and your reaction.

b. Describe an answered prayer of *not yet* or *no,* and your reaction.

Additional Scriptures
Peace, I leave with you; my peace I give you. I do not give to you as the world gives. Do not let your hearts be troubled and do not be afraid. (Jn. 14:27)

JESUS IS—OUR HELP IN FAITH OVER FEAR

There is neither Jew nor Gentile, neither slave nor free, nor is there male and female, for you are all one in Christ Jesus. (Gal. 3:28)

Beep! A horn sounded beside us, and a driver in the other vehicle waved. "There goes Fred." Jen beeped back. We all waved as my brother sped by us with traffic in the right-hand lane. Panic tightened my nerves a moment later when Mama yelled from the back seat. At the same time, I noticed a police cruiser tailed our brother's BMW SUV. The cruiser sped up to zip past an intersection caution light. *Lord, help.*

"Fred *isn't* speeding. They better not hurt my baby. Things don't always go fair for our people in these situations." Worry lined Mama's forehead. Sister and I tried to assure her everything would turn out okay. An era of blatant, public, and divisive prejudice had engendered wariness and mistrust for those sworn to protect and serve every community. Trayvon Martin and George Floyd's names are linked synonymously with hatred, prejudice, violence, and profiling of minorities. One of the most potent lessons for me as a believer and a person of color is Galatians 3:26-29.

The Apostle Paul taught the truth of grace to Galatian believers—faith in Christ's atoning death justified them (changed their status to acceptable) before God. Those baptized in Christ figuratively clothed themselves in Him. Faith conquers fear as you lean on Jesus, who promised never to leave nor forsake us.

Our brother texted to let us know he'd arrived home without incident. Life viewed via God's lens blots out bias based on race, status, religion, or other categories. Paul underscored that a Christian's spiritual identity superseded ethnic background, status, and gender. Those who, by faith, confessed Christ as Lord and Savior are God's children. The Psalmist recorded that those who trust God should never fear what man can do (Ps. 56:11).

Take part in programs that will allow you to connect and fellowship with local authorities. Pray for peace and safety in troubled areas, for survivors, victims' families, and first responders. Ask the Lord to strengthen your faith when fear threatens to bubble up.

Prayer: Jesus, be my shield of faith in a war against fear. Amen.

Jesus Is—Our Help in Faith Over Fear
Worksheet

There is neither Jew nor Gentile, neither slave nor free, nor is there male and female, for you are all one in Christ Jesus. (Gal. 3:28)

1. How can you initiate positive relationships between your family and your local police department?

2. Define *faith* in your words.

3. Describe a time when fear threatened you.

a. How did you overcome it?

b. Were there any scriptures that spoke to you?

c. Use the acrostic for fear and write words you would use to encourage someone.

F

E

A

R

JESUS IS—GOD'S SON: LISTEN TO HIM

Then a cloud appeared and covered them, and a voice came from the cloud: "This is my Son, whom I love. Listen to him!" (Mk. 9:7)

I watched a world news episode that ended with a positive story. The segment inspired hope despite earlier reports of numerous crises and tragedies. News anchors smiled, and their hands rested palms down, not clenched. Somewhere, and everywhere, people still demonstrate simple kindness, motivated by personal integrity and love. Grateful recipients expressed appreciation and notified the media. Those true stories were filled with gracious words that sweeten our souls like a honeycomb. God sent Jesus Christ as our new covenant and way home to heaven. He instructed believers to listen to the Lord.

Jesus forewarned the twelve disciples that some of them would witness the kingdom of God come with power before they died. Mark doesn't record the men's response. I imagine them mulling the information over, but no one uttered a word. Confused and awkward silence followed.

Christ led Peter, James, and John up to a high mountain six days after that announcement. The three witnessed Jesus' appearance alter. His clothing gleamed bright as blinding snow and whiter than any launderer or cold or hot water detergent could clean. Out of nowhere, two men appeared and talked with Jesus—they were Moses and Elijah. The first man symbolized the law, and the latter, prophets of old. Peter's excitement caused him to intrude on the conversation. The disciple wanted the moment to last and begged to build three dwelling places, one for each man. Had Peter fully listened and comprehended the Master's teachings thus far, he might have understood that Jesus came to fulfill the law and prophecies. One dwelling place would have sufficed.

A cloud descended and covered Elijah, Moses, and Jesus. God spoke, "This is my Son, whom I love. Listen to Him!" The New International Version Bible emphasized the insistence of God's tone by placing an exclamation point at the end of that sentence. Jesus spent time talking to and teaching the disciples. He tried to prepare them for what lay ahead. On the first day of the week, after the crucifixion, eleven disciples, bound by fear, huddled behind locked doors. Did they not believe the Lord's promise to rise in three days, or had they not listened and understood?

I post vlogs on Instagram, YouTube, and my website to fuel people's hunger for the Lord. One video references Mark 9:7. The phrase "hear Him " echoes in my soul. How often have we sat through a seminar and missed a key point by not paying attention? James, the Lord's brother, exhorts us to hear and respond (Jms. 1:22).

Set aside a specific time and place to pray and meditate on God's Word. Ask for understanding—journal thoughts and key verses that resonate. Spend the last three minutes listening to and loving the Lord.

Prayer: Lord, may I listen and learn, knowing that You are the way, the truth, and the life. All You say is for my good. Amen.

Jesus Is—God's Son: Listen to Him
Worksheet

Then a cloud appeared and covered them, and a voice came from the cloud: "This is my Son, whom I love. Listen to him!" (Mk. 9:7)

1. Read Mark 9:7 aloud. Pray and reflect on the passage. Journal your first thoughts.

2. Define *meditate* in your words.

3. What does it mean to listen with ears that hear?

Additional Scriptures
My sheep listen to my voice; I know them, and they follow me. (Jn. 10:27)

JESUS IS—THE ONE WHO HELPED THE SIFTED AND SAVED

"Simon, Simon, Satan has asked to sift all of you as wheat. (Lk. 22:31)

I'll only eat one. That's what I told myself when I threw a mini bag of milk chocolate kisses into a shopping cart. I had skipped breakfast and lunch; my stomach growled in protest. Though I'd grabbed healthy alternatives of grapes, peaches, and plums for natural sugar, all were unwashed. *Grocery stores should keep keto products on impulse displays.* By the time the cashier tallied my total, I'd eaten three more kisses. The candy quieted hunger pangs, but immediate guilt and remorse rumbled. I had failed. Again.

The Apostle Peter may have felt the same shame a time or two. The devil itched to put him through a sieve like he'd sucker-punched Job. Jesus gave Peter a heads-up. "Satan wants to sift you."

"Satan desires to sift you," Jesus warned Peter. The adversary was no respecter of persons. He sought to crush the disciples' characters, batter their faith, and make them feel scattered like trash whirled in the wind. *Sift* is derived from a Middle Eastern word, *siftan*, which means to scatter or separate. Farmers used tools and animals to beat, break, and thresh grain from wheat stalks. They tossed and sifted the chaff from wheat grain. The Lord's use of wheat sifting probably invoked familiar visual images strong enough for the disciple to comprehend. Bright hope canceled out dark despair with one word—*but.* The phrase that followed promised prayer from Jesus for the disciples to overcome.

Next, the Lord issued specific instructions to Peter to "strengthen your brothers." Satan tried to capitalize on Peter's emotional weaknesses during Jesus' last days on earth and the crucifixion. The sifting served to compel true repentance and salvation. Peter wrote letters (2 Peter) to encourage Christians to remember who and whose they were, and that He would return.

I renewed my resolve to avoid sugar and seek healthier substitutes. I manage temptation better at home than at public eateries. No matter where I go, the best results come when I tackle temptation with the Word. The Lord has promised to give us a way out (1 Cor. 10:13).

He warned Peter of the enemy's ploy and then encouraged him, "I have prayed for you."

Jesus prayed for you and me, as well (John 17).

Consider any sieving circumstances in your life as refining and smoothing. My grandmother poured flour through a sifter before baking a cake. The gadget twisted, ground, and strained coarse and lumpy grain into a smooth, fine texture. The cakes turned out light and moist. Write a letter or send a card to inspire someone who may be in a season of sifting. Express thanks often. Tell the world that you're sifted and saved.

Prayer: *Thank You, Lord, for turning the enemy's sifting into a saved refining. Amen.*

Jesus Is—The One Who Helped the Sifted and Saved
Worksheet

"Simon, Simon, Satan has asked to sift all of you as wheat." (Lk. 22:31)

1. How has Satan sifted you?

2. List ways you may have enabled the enemy easy access to attack.

3. What is Satan's ultimate goal in sifting? How can the Lord turn it into good?

Additional Scriptures
The one who does what is sinful is of the devil, because the devil has been sinning from the beginning. The reason the Son of God appeared was to destroy the devil's work. (1 Jn. 3:8)

JESUS IS — THE RESTORER

If we confess our sins, he is faithful and just and will forgive us our sins and purify us from all unrighteousness. (1 Jn. 1:9)

They emerged out of nowhere. Giant splotches of fungi perched like lily pads on a sea of dirt under my crawl space. *What if the disgusting yellow-hued intruders penetrated the foundation and walls? And its presence contaminated air quality and rendered the home unlivable?* No way. I started an exhausting Google search for exterminators. While I scrolled through website after website, glimpsing images of pests, it occurred to me that sin crept into our lives like mold. Unchecked, it spread from our mind, permeated the heart, and weakened body and spirit. Christ, our Redeemer, restored and cleansed us from the mold of transgressions.

Sin exists in every human because of our forefather Adam (Rom. 5:19). The law's limitations bound it to reveal right versus wrong and a need for correction. It couldn't provide renewal for the people. Jesus stepped down from heaven, lived among us, and suffered on a criminal's cross for our sins. Any time we mess up and confess to our Savior, He forgives our trespasses and cleanses us from unrighteousness. Our faithful and just Lord does not hold a grudge nor place a statute of limitations on forgiving. His mercy and love endure forever (Ps. 136:1)

Ventilation and exposure prevent moist, humid conditions ripe for mold growth. I've learned to monitor specific areas around the house to avoid issues in adverse weather conditions. When sunlight gleamed on those horrible yellow patches and revealed their position, I sought professional help. The mission required more work and expertise than I could manage alone.

Willing in spirit yet weak in the flesh, humanity lacked the spiritual stamina called for to wipe out sin and start anew. God sent Jesus Christ to redeem you and me — the whole world. Faith in Christ activated supernatural power to root out our sinful mold. The Apostle John advised believers to walk in the light. Both mold and sin hate light. It's the opposite of darkness. Spend more time talking and listening to the Lord. Let your actions and speech reflect a restored kingdom perspective. Speak aloud each piece of the armor of God as you put it on in the morning. Praise the Lord for the armor's protection at the close of day. The light of the Word repels lust and temptation, the co-authors of sin. Confess the mess. Jesus, our Redeemer, forgives and refreshes us anew.

Prayer: *Thank You, Jesus, for redeeming, cleaning, and restoring a sinner like me. Amen.*

Jesus Is—The Restorer
Worksheet

If we confess our sins, he is faithful and just and will forgive us our sins and purify us from all unrighteousness. (1 Jn. 1:9)

1. Explain what the word *if* means in the context of 1 John 1:9.

2. Write your definition of someone who restores.

3. Name two types of sin fungi and areas where they originate and spread.

Additional Scriptures
But if we walk in the light, as he is in the light, we have fellowship with one another, and the blood of Jesus, his Son, purifies us from all sin. (1 Jn. 1:7)

JESUS IS — THE ONE ANOINTED AT BETHANY

Then Mary took about a pint of pure nard, an expensive perfume; she poured it on Jesus' feet and wiped his feet with her hair. And the house was filled with the fragrance of the perfume. (Jn. 12:3)

Regular maintenance, gentle handling, and garage storage made my vehicle appear a newer model than its half-decade age. Occasionally, passengers have slammed doors and left trash on the seat or floor. They weren't concerned with its welfare, just enjoying a ride. I treated it with care as a blessed gift from God. Mary, sister of Lazarus, deemed Jesus a special friend and gift from God.

Jesus visited Simon the Leper's house in Bethany, two miles from Jerusalem, and ate supper with Simon, Lazarus, Mary, and Martha (Mk. 14:3). The disciples tagged along, for the Feasts of Passover and Unleavened Bread were days away. Mary understood this would be their last supper with a dear friend, chosen to die on a cross.

I attended a homegoing celebration for a childhood chum weeks before she drew her last breath. Family and friends gathered to vocalize our love and say goodbye. We wept and laughed. Hurt yet happy for her imminent heavenly healing. I wondered what emotions whirred within the three siblings while they fellowshipped, ate, and perhaps said goodbye to Jesus, friend and Savior, who resurrected Lazarus from the grave. Mary anointed His feet with spikenard oil. *Spikenard is* derived from dried roots and stems of nard, an herb of Asia, and imported from India in alabaster boxes. Households that owned a box, priced at 300 denarii or a year's wages, stored it away for special circumstances. Mary considered Jesus' death, burial, and resurrection unique. The fragrance of her sweet-smelling sacrifice filled the air from the aromatic ointment. Using her hair to wipe each foot illustrated humility. Imagine tears of sorrow and hope trickling from Mary's eyes, down her chin and mingling with the oil. 1 Samuel 2:30 promised that the Lord honors those who honor Him. Jesus ordered Mary's story to be remembered as a memorial to her and spoken in the gospel throughout the whole world (Mk. 14:7).

Prior to saving enough money to purchase my first car, I walked to work and other places. Thriving despite having less helped hone an attitude of gratitude and increased awareness of God's provision wherever I had a need. Recognize and treasure every blessing as a gift from God. Worship Him (the source), not resources. Read Matthew's eyewitness testimony of Mary anointing Jesus (Mt. 26:6-13).

Invite someone else to study. Imagine you met and interviewed Matthew and John Mark for a news story. What's the main point you'd emphasize about the One anointed at Bethany?

Prayer: Savior, may I honor and love You with free abandon, as Mary did without fear of what others think, speak, or what it costs. Amen.

Jesus is—The One Anointed at Bethany
Journal Page

Then Mary took about a pint of pure nard, an expensive perfume; she poured it on Jesus' feet and wiped his feet with her hair. And the house was filled with the fragrance of the perfume. (Jn. 12:3)

1. How can you demonstrate appreciation for a relationship and fellowship with the Lord, family, and friends?

2. Define *anoint* in your words. Why did Mary anoint Jesus?

3. How did Mary sacrifice financial gain to demonstrate love and honor for Jesus?

Additional Scriptures
When she poured this perfume on my body, she did it to prepare me for burial. (Mt. 26:12)

4. How do your interactions with Jesus reflect that you value Him?

5. List ways to fill your house with the fragrance of godly love—both your body and your address.

6. Washing feet illustrated humility. Feet washing was also a practical application. Most traveled on foot or via donkey. We can imagine that dirt roads caused dry and dusty feet. Foot washing felt as refreshing as a cold glass of water or iced tea does to us.
List the names of two difficult people in your life whose feet you'd wash.

Prayer: Lord, help me treat others with the same tender affection You give us all. Amen.

JESUS IS—HE WHO LIBERATED A GADARENE

Jesus did not let him but said, "Go home to your own people and tell them how much the Lord has done for you, and how he has had mercy on you." (Mk. 5:19)

Writers have penned tales to entertain, inform, and inspire readers. A world of harrowing heroes, demure debutantes, or maybe malicious murderers or space aliens spun suspense to captivate the mind and weave in the heart. Disciple John Mark drafted a story about how Jesus liberated a Gadarene from a graveyard and severe mental illness.

The Apostle Peter's protégé, John Mark, drew readers into an intense drama when he recorded Jesus and His disciples hit land across the shore. They stepped on Gadarene ground and met a man possessed by unclean spirits. He dwelled among the dead and decayed, and no one succeeded in restraining the unnamed man. Chains and fetters were attempted but failed. Day and night, unclean spirits tormented the man and caused him to react recklessly. He self-mutilated and ran rampant and naked among tombs and to the mountains.

The situation switched once a broken soul saw Jesus. Notice the word, *but* in verse 6. How often has the Lord altered your desperate moment of despair to high hope with that three-letter word? The unclean spirits tried to bluff and fluster Jesus by calling out His whole name. "What do You want with me, Son of the Most-High God?"

Jesus ignored their foolish ploy. "Come out of the man, you unclean spirit. What is your name?"

"Legion," announced one of the demons. "We are many."

No matter what their multitude, they begged not to be discharged out of the country. Jesus sent the demonic spirits into a nearby herd of 2,000 pigs. They stampeded down a steep place into the lake and drowned (Mk. 5:13).

Mark opted not to mention the man's name and zeroed in instead on his deliverance by the Lord. Word spread from the fearful farmers who witnessed Jesus' power. People traveled from the city and country to gawk at the miracle man. It's ironic that the restored man prayed to follow Jesus, and the answer was no. Townsfolk, afraid of Jesus' strength, pleaded with Him to get out of town. The Lord left after commissioning the liberated Gadarene to tell others his testimony.

Mark's true story testified to the Lord's infinite power and ability to heal our souls' diseases. He can speak a word, and use doctors, counselors, medicines, or therapies. Once I craved a life as a renowned author. A gentle reproof rang clear while I watched my husband re-dedicate his life to Christ. I, the regular church attendee, didn't have a relationship with Jesus. Immediate repentance and salvation followed. I still yearned to write, but the goal shifted to making Jesus famous. Share your Jesus story with others. May chains break.

Prayer: Thank You for the hills and valleys in the story of my life. Amen.

Jesus Is—He Who Liberated a Gadarene
Worksheet

Jesus did not let him, but said, "Go home to your own people and tell them how much the Lord has done for you, and how he has had mercy on you." (Mk. 5:19)

1. What's your story?

2. How powerful an effect has the Gadarene's story had on you?

3. Why did Jesus not want the Gadarene man to go with Him?

Additional Scriptures
Then they brought him a demon-possessed man who was blind and mute, and Jesus healed him, so that he could both talk and see. (Mt. 12:22)

JESUS IS — THE LORD WHO HAS RISEN

He is not here; he has risen, just as he said. Come and see the place where he lay. (Mt. 28:6)

Our Wednesday night youth class population exploded. Current student believers shared their testimonies at school. They refused to show shame when reading their Bibles between classes. Neither a curious glance nor ridicule prevented the students from praying before meals. The fruit of their labor flourished. Young guests packed a portable building behind our sanctuary, eager to learn more about Jesus, who has risen.

Jesus foretold His crucifixion and resurrection to close friends (Lk. 9:22, 17:25, 18:32-33).

Sunday morning, extremely early, several faithful women took spices to Jesus' *tomb* (sepulcher) to anoint His body. God sent two unusual occurrences to greet the ladies: A quake rocked the earth. An angel appeared in lightning white and announced a startling message, "Then go quickly and tell his disciples: 'He has risen from the dead and is going ahead of you into Galilee. There you will see him.'" (Mt. 28:7).

Fear, mingled with joy, filled the women as they hurried away in search of Jesus' eleven disciples (the twelfth, Judas Iscariot, betrayed Christ — Mt. 26:14-15).

A divine delay occurred on the women's trek. They ran into the risen Savior. "Rejoice," He declared. The ladies fell at Christ's feet in reverent worship. He comforted them and told them not to fear. "Tell my brothers to meet me in Galilee."

Mary Magdalene and her companions followed Jesus everywhere. They stood nearby, unnoticed by evil-acting elders and hired hands. Envision a scene: winded yet excited women burst into a room of bereaved men and announced, "Our friend has risen. He wants you to gather in Galilee." Matthew omitted how the eleven disciples responded. These men seemed surprised by unexpected messengers, and shocked because they'd placed Jesus in a human box.

The disciples rejoiced when they met Christ on a mountain in Galilee, though some doubted. Jesus Christ certified He had all power in heaven and earth and commissioned them to "Go make more disciples in all nations." Women were the first people to encounter our risen Lord and proclaimed the news to others. Jesus vowed victory through the Great Commission and commanded believers to disciple the world.

Children and youth grapple with giants of peer pressure, identity, and the enemy's schemes. Taking note of how friends have survived grief, family dysfunction, or avoided temptation to try illegal drugs sparks a ray of hope. I'm thankful that Cornerstone youth kindle a flame for Jesus as each one shares how He has changed their lives. Let's not hide from our past. Use it to illustrate how far you've come by faith in Christ. Pray for daily opportunities to tell your story. Be transparent and vulnerable as the Holy Spirit guides. Remember — our salvation is by grace through the risen Lord Jesus.

Prayer: Thank You, risen Savior. May I faithfully follow You and teach others. Amen.

Jesus Is — The Lord Who Has Risen
Worksheet

He is not here; he has risen, just as he said. Come and see the place where he lay. (Mt. 28:6)

1. a. Describe a moment in which you told someone or heard about a miracle.

   b. What kind of news do you typically enjoy sharing?

2. Define *disciple* and *all nations* in your words.

3. What does knowing Jesus has risen mean to you?

Additional Scriptures
Therefore, go and make disciples of all nations, baptizing them in the name of the Father and of the Son and of the Holy Spirit… (Mt. 28:19)

JESUS IS—THE UNVEILED LIGHT

But their minds were made dull, for to this day the same veil remains when the old covenant is read. It has not been removed, because only in Christ is it taken away. (2 Cor. 3:14)

A gorgeous full moon washed my front lawn in a luminous light. It caused me to delay a trip to church and compelled an awestruck gaze at Heaven's host. "Beautiful, God, just beautiful," I exclaimed before motoring on, still glimpsing its mammoth size suspended amidst a blue-black sky. Twice in the neighborhood and once at a red light, I attempted to snap quick photos without hindering traffic. Power lines, buildings, and trees obscured a clear view.

Just as those things blocked my view, disobedience and sin block a Christian's correct perception. The Apostle Paul reproved some Jews in the church at Corinth for spiritual blindness. It veiled their hearts against Jesus Christ.

Paul dug deep into the past of Israel's exodus. The apostle used a symbolic story to explain the advantages of the old covenant and the far greater blessings of the new covenant. His story started with, "God and Moses met for forty days. Moses' face radiated bright with God's glory." He wore a veil that kept the Israelites from noticing the gradual fading of temporary grandeur. The law revealed humanity's need for salvation and led to Christ. Paul reasoned that the old covenant worked as God intended. It served as a compass to point man to repentance and shone bright—for a season.

The New Covenant, Jesus Christ, fulfilled the law. Those who refused to believe and trust in the Lord as their Savior are still blinded by a veil over their hearts. The Lord liberated those who believed in Him from spiritual death. Faith in Jesus freed the Corinthian believers from false visions. Their transformed conduct and conversation cast the bright light of Jesus on family, foreigners, and non-believers.

What a blessing to be granted an unrestricted view at home and another gorgeous glimpse in our church parking lot. Stars studded the sky around an astral moon resembling a glimmering charger plate. It appeared the heavens dressed up and proclaimed the light of the Lord to all who looked.

Jesus commanded believers to "unveil" our light and let it shine (Mt. 5:14-16).

Take a moonlit drive in a country setting. Soak in the glow of heavenly gleam.

Accomplish an anonymous and sincere act of kindness for a difficult person.

Attach a card signed, "Jesus loves you."

Read the Word to nursing home residents.

May we pray that everyone invites Jesus Christ, the unveiled light, into their hearts.

Prayer: Lord, help me sparkle and unveil a light for You — The Way, the Truth, and the Life. Amen.

Jesus Is—The Unveiled Light
Worksheet

But their minds were made dull, for to this day the same veil remains when the old covenant is read. It has not been removed, because only in Christ is it taken away. (2 Cor. 3:14)

1. What life circumstances threatened to veil your view of Christ?

2. Where have you witnessed the light of understanding the Gospel shine?

3. List ways you can beam bright for Jesus. List names of those who may be veiled from the truth. Petition the Lord to remove blinders from their eyes and hearts.

Additional Scriptures
The god of this age has blinded the minds of unbelievers, so that they cannot see the light of the gospel that displays the glory of Christ, who is the image of God. (2 Cor. 4:4)

JESUS IS — MY HIDING PLACE

For you died, and your life is now hidden with Christ in God. (Col. 3:3)

Have you ever craved closing curtains on a day saturated with trials, climbing into bed, and burrowing beneath covers until a new beginning dawns? When worldly concerns, family situations, or scheduling conflicts flood my life, I've sought solace in Jesus, my hiding place.

Jesus Christ, who declared that "My Father and I are one" (Jn. 10:30), invited people with varied cares to trust and partake of His comfort, healing, and rest. Paul, an apostle hand-picked by Jesus, wrote a letter to the Colossian Christians. He proposed reinforcing spiritual understanding of their freedom in Christ and refuting false pagan teaching. *Gnostics* (a heretical group who sought salvation through secret knowledge) invaded the church. Gnosticism denied Jesus as God wrapped in humanity and incited angel worship. Paul exhorted believers to remember they died to self and were new creations. God hid (stored) His Spirit inside all who confessed belief in Jesus Christ. His death, burial, and resurrection made possible a refuge of strength and a firm foundation to shelter and find relief from trials.

Jesus has sheltered me from a barrage of emotional upheaval, grief, disappointment, and hurt. I've cried out from my truck, overwrought from an onslaught of insensitive words and actions of loved ones. Christ met me in the garage and tended to be tranquil and calm. Basking in Jesus' presence feels like a welcome homecoming of serene peace. The moment I speak His name, it is well with my soul. My shoulders relax as my mind and body lean into the goodness of the Lord. Walk or run to the One who washes out waves of worrisome tension and prompts tides of thanks. Spend time listening and sharing your heart with Jesus. Choose favorite locations such as a park, backyard, or bedroom to meet. Sense the safety and satisfaction in Jesus — our Hiding Place.

Prayer: *Thank You, Jesus, for being a sanctuary of peace, security, grace, and love. Amen.*

Jesus Is—My Hiding Place
Worksheet

For you died, and your life is now hidden with Christ in God. (Col. 3:3)

1. List some things from your past you'd rather remain concealed in the closet of "before Christ."

2. Explain in your words how a Christian's life is hidden in Jesus.

3. What does Paul mean by "For you died...."?

Additional Scriptures
I have been crucified with Christ and I no longer live, but Christ lives in me. The life I now live in the body, I live by faith in the Son of God, who loved me and gave himself for me. (Gal. 2:20)

JESUS IS—SALVATION

Brothers and sisters, my heart's desire and prayer to God for the Israelites is that they may be saved. (Rom. 10:1)

Cassie syringe-fed a miniature pup by following a veterinarian's instructions. She pressed a milk-filled tip in the little lab's mouth, determined it would taste and receive needed nourishment. I posted daily devotional vlogs on social media, craving for every contact to know Jesus as Lord and Savior. The Apostle Paul wrote letters years ago, yearning for Israel's salvation.

Paul wrote a letter to the saints who met all over Rome. Chapter 10 recorded his heart's appeal and petition to God for Israel's salvation. The apostle wrote as a parent passionate to steer overzealous yet misinformed children on the true path of knowledge. As biological descendants of Abraham, the Jews believed the law qualified them for automatic righteousness. False. The law defined sin and illuminated the dire need for a Savior. Old Testament prophets foretold the Messiah's coming centuries before He arrived (Is. 9:6, Mic. 5:2).

God's law directed people to righteousness in Christ. Those who confessed Jesus obtained salvation through Him who fulfilled the law. Paul prayed the Jews' zeal to follow God would lead them beyond self and toward the saving truth.

Centuries ago, Paul labored to spread the word that salvation comes through Christ. Today, a similar yearning drives me to write and vlog messages of encouragement. The stories I tell originate from lessons the Lord taught me. Jesus Christ descended from Heaven to seek and save the lost. Salvation came to every soul who believed and confessed Christ's identity.

Some of the milk missed the puppy's mouth. Still, the young lady stuck to guidelines and giggled in delight at each success. Months later, Pete the pup graduated from milk to dog food and continued to thrive. Paul stayed steadfast in writing letters, teaching, and preaching the gospel to Jews and Gentiles. Not all the Jewish people caught on, yet fruit was generated among Gentile believers (Rom. 11:11-15).

May we study to know God's Word and impart correct wisdom to others. Reflect Jesus in actions and speech in difficult circumstances as well as in good circumstances. Ask the Lord to grant awareness and sensitivity of opportunities to share your salvation story. Never be ashamed to give an answer for your hope—Jesus is salvation.

Prayer: Lord, from generation to generation, may we continue to testify of Your love and salvation. Speak to and through us. Amen.

Jesus Is—Salvation
Worksheet

Brothers and sisters, my heart's desire and prayer to God for the Israelites is that they may be saved. (Rom. 10:1)

1. List three things that excite you and actions that demonstrate your passion. Does being excited about God mean one knows God?

2. Paul told the Jews their zeal for God was not according to knowledge. Define *knowledge* in this context.

3. Cassie rescued a puppy and taught it to take needed nourishment. In what ways has the Lord rescued you?

4. Paul desired for Israel to come to salvation. What is the only way to salvation?

Additional Scriptures
If you declare with your mouth, "Jesus is Lord," and believe in your heart that God raised him from the dead, you will be saved. (Rom. 10:9)

JESUS IS — THE ONE WHO NEVER LEAVES US ALONE

"Never will I leave you; never will I forsake you." (Heb. 13:5b)

One moment, I soared to great spiritual heights in a worship service, and an hour later dipped low in despair at the loss of a friendship. She didn't die. The relationship fizzled. A cataclysmic storm of my friend's sorrow, both our physical exhaustion and illnesses, and miscommunication whirled into a tsunami. *Never… never…* The word spelled trouble with a capital "T," and crashed against the tide of my soul like rough waves. The last two people who promised, "I'll never leave," reneged just like Sheila.

How could I stay encouraged when family and friends seemed to topple out of my life like the domino effect? *Jesus.* His name popped into my mind immediately — the One who promised never to leave.

Over and over in the scriptures, Christ exemplified grace and unconditional love despite the pain of rejection and abandonment. Remember what happened when He traveled back home to Nazareth? The town locals uttered words of scorn in ugly disbelief after Jesus taught with eloquent wisdom at the synagogue. No banner, parade, or family reunion welcomed the hero home. Instead, people marveled at how a carpenter's child attained great intelligence. Did sadness, frustration, or anger bombard Jesus' fully human side at the people's response? I experienced all three while reading, "But Jesus said to them, 'A prophet is not without honor except in his own town and in his own home.'" (Mt. 13:57). The all-divine Lord didn't do mighty work there but remained steadfast in unconditional love.

On another occasion, a parade complete with palm branches and coats carpeting the path transpired. Crowds celebrated and escorted Jesus into Jerusalem before the Passover. Days later, the very same throng cried, "Crucify!" The Messiah pleaded from a criminal's cross, "Father, forgive them, for they know not what they do." He demonstrated in speech, actions, and reactions how to fulfill one's purpose in group settings and one-on-one. Think back to the relationship between Jesus and the twelve disciples who vowed to hang tight and remain close compadres. One outright betrayed the Lord, and three fell asleep instead of praying when He needed them most. Christ had forewarned and encouraged Peter, "Satan desires to sift you as wheat. I have prayed that your faith may not fail. When you recover, strengthen your brothers" (Lk. 22:31-32 paraphrased).

Solitary time in a desert taught Jesus to lean and depend on the Father in heaven. He fought the enemy with the Word and kept a goal-oriented mindset. Love covers a multitude of sins. The Lord used a time of separation between my friend and me to reveal that: 1) Believers sometimes disagree yet always love one another; and 2) Whatever the chaos or mess from flesh or the enemy, Jesus' power can transform it into a glorious message.

Set aside time with Jesus for spiritual recalibration. Studying the Word derives direction, balance, and contentment. Read it with an intent to hear from the Lord. Pray continually in adoration, confession, thanksgiving, and supplication. Live service-driven. Remember that Jesus pledged, "Surely, I am with you always, even until the very end of the age." We're never alone.

Prayer: *Lord, our promises to You and one another often fail. Thank You for never leaving us in the best and the worst times. Amen.*

Jesus Is—The One Who Never Leaves Us Alone
Worksheet

"Never will I leave you; never will I forsake you." (Heb. 13:5b)

1. Describe a time when you have experienced loneliness.

2. How does knowing Christ as a constant companion benefit you?

3. Use the acrostic below to list words of comfort and assurance sensed in "never alone."

N=

E=

V=

E=

R=

A=

L=

O=

N=

E=

Additional Scriptures
Have I not commanded you? Be strong and courageous. Do not be afraid; do not be discouraged, for the LORD *your God will be with you wherever you go."* (Josh. 1:9)

JESUS IS — THE ONE WHO CLEANED ME UP

Therefore, if anyone is in Christ, the new creation has come: The old has gone, the new is here! (2 Cor. 5:17)

A popular social media site prompted patrons to post pictures of joyous events, popular hangouts, and people from the past. While the sights, clothing, and hairstyles from back in the day were fun to browse, I'm grateful to no longer live or identify as my past. The old has been washed away in the cleansing blood of Jesus. The Apostle Paul once described himself as the "chief of sinners." An infamous road encounter with Jesus compelled Paul to renounce a former lifestyle, live for Christ, and proclaim, "The old has gone, and the new is here!"

Persecutor and murderer Saul transformed into peaceful Apostle Paul, serving the same Christ he formerly slaughtered men and women for believing in. The 180-degree change occurred because the zealous martyr encountered Jesus on one of his murderous missions. Imagine pure light from heaven suddenly shining brighter than the noon sun beaming on you. Saul hit the ground. Do you suppose a mixture of fear and humility forced him there?

A voice roaring with power and authority called Saul by name and thundered forth a question, "Why are you persecuting Me? I am Jesus." How many times have our words and actions persecuted the Savior? How do we fix the wrong? Surrender like Saul: "Lord, what do You want me to do?"

Three days of fasting from food and drink, plus being struck blind, primed Saul's heart to soak in words from God's servant Ananias. Immediately after receiving the Holy Ghost, scales of blindness fell from his eyes. He could see and wasted no time in getting baptized. The old man passed away. Saul no longer desired to live and think in the past. A new creation in Christ with a new name, Paul preached the gospel with great zeal.

An Instagram post encouraged us to push through despite the current storms of pain and trials. I glimpsed it while struggling to drink water, having no appetite or energy, and wanting to give up on writing. That message recalled God's Word and renewed passion for a fresh start. I'm grateful for the testimonies of men and women like Paul. God repurposed ordinary, imperfect sinners into transformed, redeemed ambassadors for Christ. Their stories inspire hope and motivate us to press on. Are you looking for a new look or want a fresh start? Begin on the inside. Ask Jesus to come into your heart and mold you into a new creation.

Some people prefer not to talk about difficult life circumstances and lock them in the past. Meditating on the Word taught me to testify about the Lord's transforming power in my life. I spent much of my life yearning to overcome shyness and seeking acceptance. One Wednesday night, an associate minister introduced me to Jesus. The chains were undone! I started boasting about the Lord and forgot about the hurtful names of *four eyes* and *dark-skinned*. Sharon no longer lived for the flesh. Christ lived in me.

Tell your story repeatedly. Celebrate your date of rebirth with family and friends. Take a calendar to a gathering of those you want to witness to. Invite them to mark a special day when they viewed Jesus at work while sharing the story. Jesus Christ can change anyone into a new creation.

Prayer: *Lord, make me over from the inside out into who You created me to be. Amen.*

Jesus Is—The One Who Cleaned Me Up
Worksheet

Therefore, if anyone is in Christ, the new creation has come: The old has gone, the new is here! (2 Cor. 5:17)

1. List all the ways you have felt renewed in the past. How long did the sensation of renewal last?

2. Explain in your words how to become a new creation in Christ. Is it based on emotions and feelings or faith in Jesus?

3. What's the number one characteristic of a new creation according to 2 Corinthians 5:17?

Additional Scriptures
… that God was reconciling the world to himself in Christ, not counting people's sins against them. And he has committed to us the message of reconciliation. (2 Cor. 5:19)

JESUS IS—THE ULTIMATE SACRIFICE

But God demonstrates his own love for us in this: While we were still sinners, Christ died for us. (Rom. 5:8)

Did you know that loving others right where they are exemplifies grace? Don't criticize. Care. Pray for the Lord to transform heart and soul. God demonstrated this love by sending Jesus, His only begotten Son, to die on the cross while we were yet sinners.

Holy God, who can abide no transgression, has judged humanity guilty. In an extraordinary show of unconditional love, the Judge acted as defense lawyer and bail bondsman. He substituted someone else to pay for our punishment. The job called for a special individual. Few stood in line, applying to sacrifice their life for a good person, let alone a bunch of lawbreakers. One sinless Son stepped down from heaven, heeding His Father's call. Jesus. He so loved the world that He uttered not one complaint against unchanged hearts, while enduring incomprehensible pain.

May we pay forward Jesus' sacrificial love and selfless service, and greet others with Christmas cheer all through the year. Pray for those you meet who seem difficult to get along with. Everyone has a story. Consider each day and circumstance as a teaching moment. What would Jesus do in a particular situation? Remember how He paid the ultimate sacrifice for all.

Prayer: Jesus, we can't understand the depth of pain you took for us. "Thank You" seems so inadequate, yet we are thankful. Amen.

Jesus Is—The Ultimate Sacrifice
Worksheet

But God demonstrates his own love for us in this: While we were still sinners, Christ died for us. (Rom. 5:8)

1. Define *sinner* in your words.

2. List ways you can love others as Christ loves us.

3. How can you demonstrate your love of Jesus to God?

4. Is there someone you're praying would extend you more grace? Do you need God's help to give grace to someone else? List the name(s) and pray in faith.

Additional Scriptures

For you know the grace of our Lord Jesus Christ, that though he was rich, yet for your sake he became poor, so that you through his poverty might become rich. (2 Cor. 8:9)

JESUS IS— NICODEMUS'S TEACHER BY NIGHT

He came to Jesus at night and said, "Rabbi, we know that you are a teacher who has come from God. For no one could perform the signs you are doing if God were not with him." (Jn. 3:2)

Medline[8] cites *in vitro fertilization* as the joining of a woman's fertile egg and a man's sperm in a laboratory dish. The Latin word *in vitro* (within the glass) means happening outside the body. The process for many hopeful parents today might seem as daunting and unrealistic as Jesus' answer to Nicodemus back then. "Unless a man is born again, he can't see the kingdom of God" (Jn. 3:3).

Crowds packed the city of Jerusalem for Passover. No telling what criminals roamed among them, yet something beyond his comprehension compelled Nicodemus, a law expert, to risk meeting Jesus at night. Maybe night illustrated the dark state of the Pharisees' faith. The others in their sect refused to acknowledge the teacher as Messiah, but Nicodemus couldn't deny that God sent Jesus. Visualize the swishing of his robe hem and rapid staccato of an anxious heart as he hurried along. Imagine that Jesus stepped forward and spoke, "Shalom." The religious hypocrite, who'd judged kings before, as a member of the elite Sanhedrin (Greek for assembly), now stood unaware before the King of kings. The correct words poured forth, "Rabbi (Teacher), we know You came from God. No man can perform the miracles you're doing unless God were with Him."

Ever interested in our salvation, Jesus' reply aimed at teaching the true path: "You must be born again."

That answer confused the Pharisee, who listened with ears incapable of comprehending the message. Hence, his following words, "How can a grown man go back into his mother's womb and be born?" The wisdom of God is foolish to a man without faith.

The Lord explained a second birth, not from the watery womb of a mother, but as an inner spiritual change. The teacher planted seeds of knowledge in an inquisitive student. Could they not take root in the hard ground of tradition? Were they choked out by weeds of care over prestige and power? I think the same spiritual blindfold that caused Nicodemus to meet under cover still chained him to traditions and pride in his present life. Jesus often advised, "He who has ears to hear, let him hear," to remind recipients of the Word to listen, trust, and obey. Had the law expert and ruler done so, he might have repented and begged the teacher sent by God to baptize him.

A 2021 Mayo Clinic article lauded in vitro fertilization (IVF) as the most effective form of assisted reproductive technology. The process grants another option to those unable to get pregnant by the usual method. No matter how you were physically conceived, spiritual repentance and rebirth transpire in the heart and mind. Confess your dependence on and faith in the Lord. Study, savor, and follow the Word. Devote quality time to prayer. Fellowship with those who encourage and inspire growth.

Prayer: Lord, thank You for Your willingness to meet us anytime and anywhere. Amen.

---

[8] In vitro fertilization (IVF): MedlinePlus Medical Encyclopedia

Jesus Is—Nicodemus's Teacher by Night
Worksheet

He came to Jesus at night and said, "Rabbi, we know that you are a teacher who has come from God. For no one could perform the signs you are doing if God were not with him." (Jn. 3:2)

1. What has Jesus done in your life to cause you to know He comes from God?

2. List some good news you have heard at night.

3. When in the past did you desire to speak up or ask a question, and fear thwarted you?

4. Use the acrostic below to create positive words that override fear and pride:

F=

E=

A=

R=

*

P=

R=

I=

D=

E=

Additional Scriptures

What you have said in the dark will be heard in the daylight, and what you have whispered in the ear in the inner rooms will be proclaimed from the roofs. (Lk. 12:3)

JESUS IS — THE TRUE VINE

"I am the true vine, and my Father is the gardener. (Jn. 15:1)

I pulled, tugged, and cut out a small cluster of watermelon vines, some still heavy with fruit, from a flower bed. Despite days of oppressive temperatures above 105 degrees, their roots clung beneath the soil. Just as the vines held fast in the soil, Christ is the firm foundation for believers to grasp and dwell.

Jesus used a job still typical in this century to illustrate how believers should abide in Him. The story revolved around a farmer or vinedresser (God), a genuine vine (Jesus), and believers (branches). Notice that "I am" at the beginning signified Christ as one with the Father, whom He recognized as Head authority. Every branch (all who believed) came to God through Jesus. They grew from the fertilizer of the Word and produced fruit (good works that drew more people to Christ and glorified God). Seasonal pruning through painful afflictions cuts off dead and inactive limbs. Those fell to the ground and dried and were only useful for firewood. The healthy branches remained, waxed stronger, and produced more fruit. The word *clean* means saved in this context.

Vines retard weed growth and prevent soil erosion. As a plant, a vine gleans nutrition from the soil to flourish, sprout vibrant limbs, and produce lush leaves. May you and I cling to Jesus and soak up spiritual sustenance. Focusing on the True Vine eliminates unwanted briars of negative thoughts and sows seeds of faith. We're empowered to glorify God by bearing the good fruit of the Spirit. Examples might include patient service, love for those considered difficult, and putting others' interests first. Stand ready and willing to share the good news of Jesus and your redemption story with everyone who asks.

Prayer: *Lord, may I hang on to You, knowing that You are the Vine of life from here to eternity. Amen.*

Jesus is — the True Vine
Worksheet

"I am the true vine, and my Father is the gardener. (Jn. 15:1)

1. Describe what you think when you view the first two words of John 15:1 above, "I am."

2. Define *true* in your words.

3. Who does the true vine represent?

4. How does God the Father care for you as a branch in His garden?

Additional Scriptures
"I am the vine; you are the branches. If you remain in me and I in you, you will bear much fruit; apart from me, you can do nothing. (Jn. 15:5)

JESUS IS—THE ONE WHO CANCELLED OUR DEBT

When he had received the drink, Jesus said, "It is finished." With that, he bowed his head and gave up his spirit. (Jn. 19:30)

The latest statement on my credit cards read zero dollars.

Paid.

What a relief to no longer have that burden. It was done. As a sinner, I also owe a massive spiritual debt just like you, my friend, and the whole world, too. Jesus came from Heaven to seek, save the lost, and fully satisfy our sin debt. The last words He spoke on the cross were, "It's finished."

Beaten and mocked, Jesus carried a cross on a path from Jerusalem called Via Dolorosa to where He'd soon hang at Golgotha. He hung there as soldiers cast lots for His clothing. At last, Christ cried, "I thirst." No one rushed forward with a dip of cold water. Instead, the Bible records the Lord's last drink as vinegar on hyssop. He took it, then spoke three words, "It is finished." *Tetelestai* means paid in full and is the Greek word for that phrase. Jesus paid the price for our past, present, and future sins. Therefore, there is no condemnation for those who confess Christ as our Savior (Rom. 8:1).

Since Jesus' blood washed away our stain of guilt (Is. 1:18), God no longer remembers our sins. If God the Father forgets the past, why can't we forgive ourselves and walk in the newness of life?

Note-burning parties were once popular when homeowners paid off their mortgages. Setting the installment plan aflame symbolized a done deal. Live each new day in celebration of your debt cancellation by Christ. Consider your body a living sacrifice in choices and actions to draw others to Him and glorify God. Adopt a permanent attitude of gratitude for each blessing.

Prayer: Jesus, You obeyed even to death on the cross for a sinner such as I. I'm grateful. Amen.

Jesus Is—The One Who Cancelled Our Debt
Worksheet

When he had received the drink, Jesus said, "It is finished." With that, he bowed his head and gave up his spirit. (Jn. 19:30)

1. What debt do you owe Jesus?

2. What does Jesus' death on the cross mean to you?

3. Does someone owe you a debt that you could stamp *paid in full*? Would you? Why or why not?

4. Why does verse 30 above state that "Jesus gave up the spirit," instead of "He died"?

Additional Scriptures

For God so loved the world that he gave his one and only Son, that whoever believes in him shall not perish but have eternal life. (Jn. 3:16)

JESUS IS—THE ONE WHO PURSUED US

A few days later, when Jesus again entered Capernaum, the people heard that he had come home. (Mk. 2:1)

This past spring, Sassy found a weak spot in the backyard fencing and managed to dig out. We found her running through the woods with another dog. I purchased dog defense, anti-dig aids, and repaired the fence. The smart aleck mastiff waited until I went to bed and searched for yet another area in the aged wiring. She'd gotten a taste of the outside world and a stranger to explore with. We hunted for her for days. Matthew recorded a parable of Jesus about a man who lost one of his hundred sheep. He left the ninety-nine and went after the one gone astray.

Jesus returned to Capernaum, an area where He'd healed many of various diseases and taught with authority the Jews had never heard before. Enthusiastic crowds who sought miracles packed the city, thus halting the Lord's teaching and preaching there on His first visit. Determined to pursue lost souls, Jesus trekked back from the desert and preached the message of repentance and salvation. In the parable of the lost sheep, He is the Shepherd who pursues unbelievers (lost sheep) and leads them into the fold of eternal life through repentance and redemption in Him by the gift of grace.

The American Kennel Club suggested that boredom, stress relief, or genetics might cause dogs to dig. Sassy's cousin, Jax, a one-year-old bulldog, started visiting for playdates. Sweet Jax huddled up close. My seven-year-old fur girl couldn't make a move without him. When he left, she retired under the porch at peace to be home sweet home. Let the Lord catch you. Rehearse the promises in God's word. Pray to point people to Christ.

Prayer: *Savior, like a Shepherd, You chased and caught Your unlearned sheep. Thank You for teaching and saving us. Amen.*

Jesus Is—The One Who Pursued Us
Worksheet

A few days later, when Jesus again entered Capernaum, the people heard that he had come home. (Mk. 2:1)

1. When was the last time you were pursued? Was it a positive event?

2. What does it mean to know that Jesus chased after you?

3. Who or what have you chased after in your lifetime?

A. Did you reach the goal?

B. Did it satisfy the longing within?

4. List the differences you note between a physical miracle and an eternal salvation.

Additional Scriptures
Jesus went through all the towns and villages, teaching in their synagogues, proclaiming the good news of the kingdom and healing every disease and sickness. (Mk. 9:35)

JESUS IS — MARY'S BABY

You will conceive and give birth to a son, and you are to call him Jesus. (Lk. 1:31)

21st century expectant mothers mark their pending arrival with photo sessions, gender reveals, and baby showers. Labor and delivery may take place in a sterile room with OB/GYN and other medical staff or in a special birthing room, still with medical personnel, and surrounded by family. Centuries ago, a virgin teen named Mary delivered her baby in a barn. Her espoused husband attended the momentous occasion with farm animals nearby.

May we not miss the miracles that made Mary's baby's birth extraordinary. Modern-day couples choose a time and place to share exciting news of an addition to their family. Mary and Joseph were a betrothed couple, not living together, and someone else announced news of Mary's conception. The "someone else" was not a member of the family but an angel sent from God.

Angels didn't just pop in for a friendly hello. His sudden appearance may have caused initial fright. Greetings of favor sent from an extraordinary God shocked a Jewish teen who perhaps deemed her life unremarkable. "How could this be?" Mary questioned, quite confused. "I'm espoused to Joseph and have never known a man in this physical way," the young virgin declared. The angel reassured Mary that God had favored her as the human vessel to carry and deliver His Son, planted inside her by the Holy Spirit. "With God, all things are possible."

He offered the fantastic news of an older cousin named Elizabeth for further proof. Once thought barren, Elizabeth had conceived a son and had just concluded her sixth month of pregnancy.

How amazing to view the blessed Trinity at work as Jesus entered the earth from heaven to save us. The Holy Spirit overshadowed Mary by the power of God, and she conceived a child. Contemporary prospective parents search for a perfect name. The angel relayed a name to Mary and Joseph, given by God. "Call Him Jesus. He shall be great and named the Son of the Most High." Mary's response exemplified faith in God. "Behold a maidservant of the Lord. Be it unto me as you have said."

What nuggets can we glean from the not-so-ordinary birth of Mary's baby? The same power of God that formed baby Jesus also created you. You're fearfully and wonderfully made for a purpose (Ps. 139:14, Jer. 29:11).

Just as Jesus came to earth to seek and save the lost from eternal sin, God created us with talents and gifts to build up His people and glorify His name. He knows the very number of hairs on your head. His love runs deep enough to sacrifice His only begotten Son for you. The truth of John 3:16 pierced my heart in 2001. I hadn't volunteered my twenty-two-year-old son. Bipolar disorder blurred his spiritual focus and robbed us of his presence. Ijuan confessed Christ as his Savior seven weeks before dying. God sent His Son so my child, you, and I can live sin- and pain-free with Him (Lk. 12:7, Jn. 3:16).

Study the Word and discern the truth. Revere the Lord as the Jewish teen did and recognize messages via the Word, the Spirit, or vessels. God used what the world deemed weak or foolish to work miracles. Israel awaited a king to emerge in royal apparel to rescue them from Roman oppression, not a baby born in a barn. You and every baby originated from God's power. How will God use you or your baby?

Prayer: *Jesus, may we obey our call from the Father and act in faith as You and Your earthly parents* *demonstrated. Amen*

Jesus Is—Mary's Baby
Worksheet

You will conceive and give birth to a son, and you are to call him Jesus. (Lk. 1:31)

1. List ways to encourage a baby (young child) to fulfill their purpose.

2. What truths have you discovered about your birth from this devotional?

3. Use the acrostic, *Baby*, and write down as many words of affirmation for each letter as possible. Practice utilizing those words in sincere encouragement to those whose path you cross.

B=

A=

B=

Y=

Additional Scriptures
Today in the town of David, a Savior has been born to you; he is the Messiah, the Lord. (Lk. 2:11)

JESUS IS — THE WORD

In the beginning was the Word, and the Word was with God, and the Word was God. (Jn. 1:1)

I studied a detailed human ear, nose, and throat diagram. A nurse practitioner strolled in and noticed me staring at the chart.

"Fascinating.

"Yes. It's amazing how God interweaves all these intricate parts together." I returned her smile.

"It makes you wonder how anyone could doubt His existence, knowing the miracle of humanity's makeup," Nurse Practitioner Harden sighed. The Apostle John wrote an evangelistic account of the gospel so saints and the world may believe Jesus is the incarnate (God in flesh) and the inspired Word.

Bible scholars noted that four of Jesus' disciples penned gospels on His life, each from a different perspective. Matthew detailed Jesus' earthly genealogy through David and the Old Testament. Mark followed the Messiah's background in Nazareth and highlighted servanthood. Luke linked Christ's ancestry to Adam, whose sin compelled our need for the sinless Savior. John wrapped up the four-part gospel, demonstrating the origin of Jesus, who hailed from heaven.

"In the beginning..." John's first three words pointed back to Genesis Chapter 1 and left no room for guessing. The Word existed long ago. Next, we're told the Word was with God. Remember in Genesis when He said, "Let us make mankind in our image" (Gen. 1:26)?

John tops the delectable news with the sweetest cherry. "The Word was God." Verse 14 spelled the truth out in layman's terms for those who struggled with the first verse. "The Word became flesh and made his dwelling among us. We have seen his glory, the glory of the one and only Son, who came from the Father, full of grace and truth." One of Jesus' titles is *Logos,* which is defined as *word* or *speech.* The phrase "the Word of God" occurred in the Old Testament over 1,200 times to refer to the message of God. Perhaps that's why Bible scholars refer to the One who expresses and communicates the Word as Logos. Jesus descended from heaven and took on human form. He who knew no sin was fully human and fully divine. To deny either means total disbelief in Jesus, the Word.

Nerves, tubes, and other tissues connect the ear, nose, and throat. I learned how sinus allergies and infections trigger the three organs from the inside out. What we say, think, and how we act reflect whether we believe in God and Jesus. You can only receive a relationship and fellowship with the Holy Spirit once you confess and believe in Christ as your Lord and Savior. John sought for every saved person and the world to know Jesus' true identity. The ball has fallen into our court to make Jesus known and famous. First, get to know the One you're campaigning for. Second, understand it's a forever job, so pray for a made-up mind to represent the Lord 24/7. Last, take time to sit and soak in His love for you.

Prayer: *Jesus, may I study You, the Word, and do all I can to make You famous. Amen.*

Jesus Is—The Word
Worksheet

In the beginning was the Word, and the Word was with God, and the Word was God. (Jn. 1:1)

1. Define the phrase "In the beginning" in John 1:1.

2. Who is the Word?

3. Write about your beginning with Jesus as your Savior. If you haven't made the step, write about your future plans and why Jesus may or may not be included.

Additional Scriptures
I and the Father are one. (Jn. 10:30)

JESUS IS—THE TRUTH

Jesus answered, "I am the way, and the truth, and the life. No one comes to the Father except through me. (Jn. 14:6)

Almost every group organizes with a mission or goals and a statement of truth they stand on. Gathering in agreement does not guarantee truth. The pure truth originated from the One who created heaven, earth, and all within. Jesus prayed to the Father, "Your word is truth."

Nelson's Bible Dictionary defined *truth* as conformity to fact, faithfulness to a standard, and the moral and personal characteristic of God. Scripture throughout the Bible proclaims, "God is truth. Your law is truth." Isaiah referred to the Lord as "the God of truth." Jesus reigns as the only begotten Son and second person of the Holy Trinity. He is God cloaked in humanity who dwelt among us. John confirmed Christ's identity: "In the beginning was the Word, and the Word was with God, and the Word was God" (Jn. 1:1).

Jews surrounded Jesus on Solomon's porch and sought His identity. He certified, "I and my Father are one" (Jn. 10:30).

Jesus prepared eleven disciples for His passion and departure back to heaven. "Let not your heart be troubled. I am the way, the truth, and the life. I will send the Comforter, who is the Spirit of truth. He will guide you. I came forth from the Father and will return to the Father."

Search social media and watch one segment of the world evening news. You'll get a gist of what's considered truth in the world and our nation. Popular opinion and majority rule may appear to outweigh God's Word, but victory belongs to Jesus. The optimum way to live as our Manufacturer intended depends on studying and obeying the truth. Let's evaluate the missions of clubs and groups we've joined. Make sure they pursue and present pure truth. Jesus is the way, the truth, and the life, and our pathway to eternal peace with God.

Prayer: Thank You, Jesus, for being the truth and pathway of peace to God. Amen.

Jesus Is—The Truth
Worksheet

Jesus answered, "I am the way and the truth and the life. No one comes to the Father except through me. (Jn. 14:6)

1. List beliefs you trusted in the past.

2. What hope did these beliefs inspire?

3. How will you share the truth of Jesus?

Additional Scriptures
Instead, speaking the truth in love, we will grow to become in every respect the mature body of him who is the head, that is, Christ. (Eph. 4:15)

ABOUT THE AUTHOR

SD (Sharon) Simms resides in East Texas and thrives on being an agent of joy for Jesus. She graduated from Tyler Commercial College with a Fashion Merchandising Degree, gained twenty years of practical and continuing education in criminal justice, and is certified in suicide intervention. Sharon joined ACFW-East Texas under Joy Massenburge and started learning the craft of writing. She attended meetings, held positions as chaplain and secretary, and purchased and studied writing resources.

Sharon is a grateful believer in Jesus Christ who adores family, friends, and people in general and serving God. She is a member of ACFW national and ACFW-DFW local, AWSA, Word Weavers International and the 540-writing community. Sharon posts daily devotional vlogs on *www.sharondsimms.com*, YouTube, and Instagram. Published works include three online articles, one for *Christianity.com*, *Ibelieve.com*, and *Biblestudytools.com*, a devotion posted on Arise Daily, and one pictorial devotion for the Upper Room. The Lord Is… a Forty-Day Devotional from the Lessons from My Father Series, released March 2025 under Mt Zion Ridge Press.

THANK YOU!

Thank you for reading this book from Mt. Zion Ridge Press.

If you enjoyed the experience, learned something, gained a new perspective, or made new friends through the story, could you do us a favor and write a review on Goodreads or wherever you bought the book?

Thanks! We and our authors appreciate it.

We invite you to visit our website, MtZionRidgePress.com, and explore other titles in fiction and non-fiction. We always have something coming up that's new and off the beaten path.

And please check out our podcast, **Books on the Ridge,** where we chat with our authors and give them a chance to share what was in their hearts while they wrote their book, as well as fun anecdotes and glimpses into their lives and experiences and the writing process. And we always discuss a vital topic: *Tea!*

You can listen to the podcast on our website or find it at most places where podcasts are available online. Please subscribe so you don't miss a single episode!

Thanks for reading. We hope you come back soon!